101 WOMEN'S BASKETBALL DRILLS

Theresa Grentz
Gary Miller

ISBN: 1-57167-083-1
Library of Congress Catalog Card Number: 96-72014

Book Layout and Diagrams: Antonio J. Perez
Cover Design: Deborah M. Bellaire
Cover Photos: Courtesy of the *Daily Illini*

Coaches Choice Books is an imprint of:

Sagamore Publishing, Inc.
P.O. Box 647
Champaign, IL 61824-0647
(800) 327-5557
(217) 359-5940
Fax: (217) 359-5975
Web Site: http//www.sagamorepub.com

This book is dedicated to my mother and father, Christina and John Shank. My father taught me to never give up, and my mother taught me to always find a way. Much love to two of the most influential people in my life.

ACKNOWLEDGMENTS

A very special thank you to Gary Miller for his time, patience, and understanding in the completion of this basketball drill book.

To my players over the years who have shown me a continued love for the game of basketball.

To my coaching staff, Kathleen McConnell, LaVonda Wagner, and Renee Reed, for their continued support and loyalty.

A special thanks to my former assistant coach, Kathleen Shanahan Shank, for her continued support and loyalty and also for her contribution and compiling of many of these drills over the years of our working relationship.

I have to thank Sandi Landeck for her understanding, dedication, typing, and motivation to get this project completed.

CONTENTS

FOREWORD

When Theresa Grentz asked me to pen the foreword of her first published book, I was admittedly stunned. After all, mine is merely one of thousands of lives this remarkable woman has touched throughout her 23-year coaching career. Therefore, I write on behalf of *all* the family, friends, players, and coaches who have had the incredible privilege of knowing and learning from one of America's all-time greatest basketball coaches, Theresa Grentz.

As I began as an assistant coach for Theresa Grentz four years ago, I was immediately gripped by her intense sense of focus and vision. She was—and is—a woman on a mission. There is no room for mediocrity, no room for second place. Indeed, her drive and competitiveness are second to none.

It did not take long for me to realize that I was working for not merely a coach, but for an engineer—an engineer in the sense of a master builder, capable of integrating a number of parts into a synergistic whole. Off the court, Theresa carries out the roles of mother, motivator, entrepreneur, and public figure, each with equal ease. On the court, her talent lies in assigning and integrating the roles of her players so that the whole is greater than the sum of its parts. An important aspect of this talent is Theresa's ability to maximize individual talent and to draw forth the best from those around her. While some of this is done through her charisma and motivational techniques, the rest is accomplished through her sheer knowledge of the game and her experience with all levels of players. Whether working with Olympians or young basketball campers, Theresa knows what it takes to succeed.

A true visionary, Theresa has led the ranks in the progress of women's basketball since her days as a three-time All-American at Immaculata College. Since that time, Theresa has claimed every honor existing today for a collegiate basketball coach. Not only did her Rutgers University team win a national championship in 1982, but she was also named the Converse National Coach of the Year, a two-time Kodak District II Coach of the Year, a four-time Atlantic 10 Coach of the Year, the Head Coach of the United States for the World Championships, the Goodwill Games, and ultimately, the 1992 Olympics. Along the way she has produced three first-team All-Americans, including Sue Wicks, who received the honor for three consecutive years.

Through it all, Theresa has never lost touch with young, potential players and a firm belief in fundamentals. Of course, that's where it all begins. Consequently, Theresa's first book consists of the drills and techniques that she has used to develop skilled, successful athletes. There is no doubt that these will be useful to you as you plan your practices and create individual workouts. However, as you finish this book, I know you will be left wanting more. I can only hope that *101 Women's Basketball Drills* will tide you over until the "engineer" returns with another book filled with her wisdom and insight on teamwork, roles, motivation, and an undying urgency to succeed. In the words of Theresa Grentz, "Dare to be great!"

Foreword prepared by Renee Reed. Renee, currently an assistant women's basketball coach at the University of Illinois, is a 1993 Dartmouth College graduate and a Phi Beta Kappa. She has also served as an assistant women's basketball coach at Rutgers University where she earned her M. Ed.

PREFACE

It is my hope that his book will provide those who are reading it with an insight into the instructional part of this great game of basketball. This is a compilation of some of my favorite drills that I have found to be both instructional and developmental. Over the years many of my players have contributed greatly to the progression and fine tuning of these drills. Some of the best drills were the ones that they later told me they hated to do; and these are some of those drills that I would like to share with you.

As the coach and leader of your team, it is important that you remember that you are the artist for how your team is going to look once they take the floor. They are an extension of your personality. Therefore, be creative; use the drills in this book as a design or guideline. Change, implement, and advance these drills for the betterment of your players.

Here's wishing you much success and happiness in one of the finest professions—teaching.

—Theresa Grentz

TERMINOLOGY KEY

Baseline: The line that extends from sideline to sideline behind each basket of the court.

Division line: The line extending from sideline to sideline dividing the court into two equal parts.

Elbow: The area in which each side line of the free throw lane intersects the free throw line.

High post: The area between the two elbows at the corners of the free throw lane and the area outside the free throw line inside the free throw circle.

Key: The area enclosed by the two side lines of the free throw lane and the top half of the free throw circle.

Low post: The area outside the free throw lane on each side of the basket extending from the plane of the backboard to approximately halfway to the free throw line.

Mid post: The area of transition between the low post area and the high post area.

Rebounding ring: A device used in rebounding drills attached to the rim to increase the chances of a missed basket.

Sideline: The line that extends from baseline to baseline along the side of the court.

Spin technique: A basic movement technique for getting an inside position. This move is a counter for the swim technique. When an opponent responds to what she believes to be a swim technique by moving over to block out, the player simply spins off the opponent's back and rolls directly into the desired rebounding position. The player uses her opponent's momentum against her.

Swim technique: A basic movement technique for getting an inside position. Once a player knows which direction she is going for a rebound, for example, she "swims" (i.e., throws her inside arm and leg through) past her opponent, as if her opponent's arm and shoulder were in water in a pool. The emphasis is to thrust her high, "swimming" arms past her opponent and step over her opponent's closest leg with her inside leg in order to propel her past her opponent to a desired spot on the court.

DIAGRAM KEY

G = guard player
W = wing player
HP = high post player
R = rebounder
P = shooting player
C = coach
X = defensive player
O = offensive player

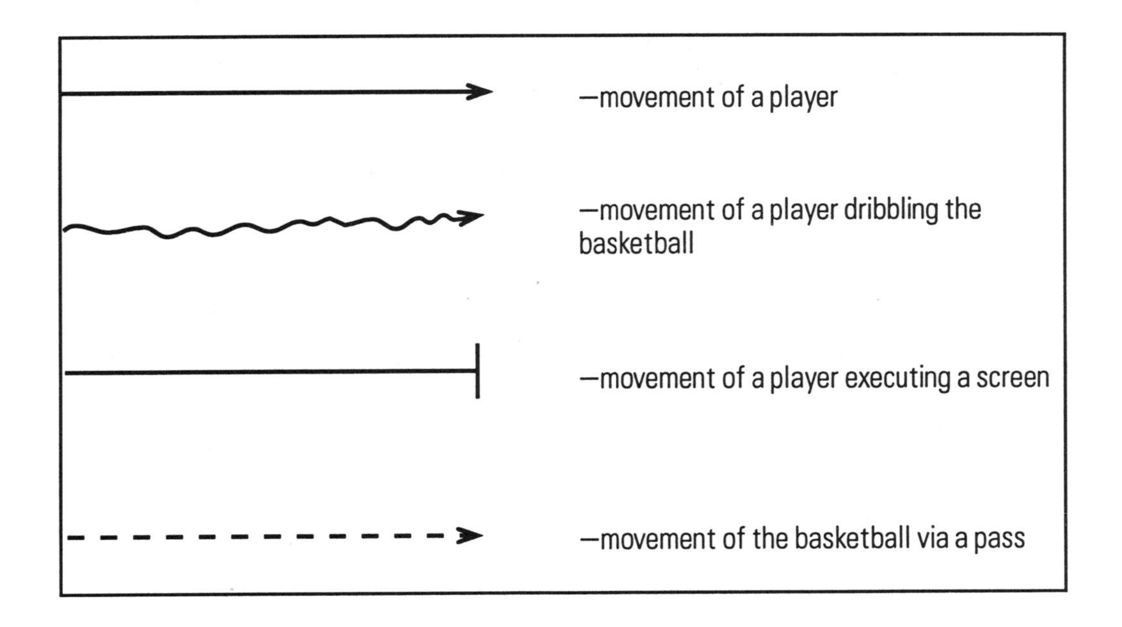
—movement of a player
—movement of a player dribbling the basketball
—movement of a player executing a screen
—movement of the basketball via a pass

BALL-HANDLING DRILLS

Drill #1: Zig Zag

Objective: To teach ball-handling skills.

Description: Divide the team into three groups and position them on the baseline outside the court. Each line should have a basketball. The first person in line is on defense and defends against the dribbler the entire length of the court. Each line operates in approximately one-third of the width of the court. The dribbler works within this area and moves the ball down the court by executing the appropriate dribble according to the defensive position. A crossover, behind the back or between the legs dribble may be used to proceed down the court.

Coaching Points:

- A player should work on those dribbling techniques that enable her to evade the defense and to best protect the ball.
- Not becoming predictable in evading the pressure of defense should be emphasized.

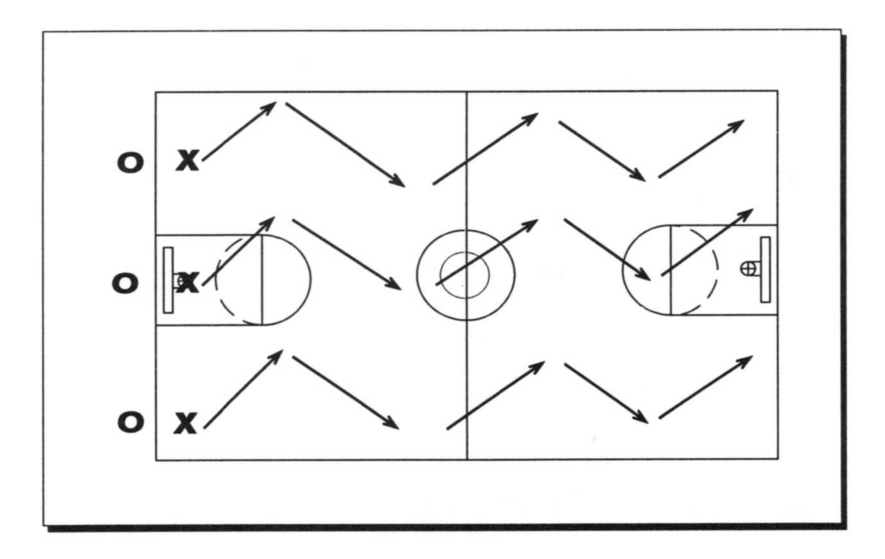

Drill #2: Maze Dribble

Objective: To improve ability and enhance confidence in dribbling skills.

Description: Position four to six players on each side of the lane facing the half court line. Each player should have one foot on the side line of the free throw lane and the other foot inside the lane. These players should be equally spaced and positioned to provide a maze for the dribbler to go through. The dribbler begins at the top of the key and attempts to dribble through the maze to the baseline and return to the top of the key without losing the basketball. The players along the lane may bat the ball away from the dribbler with their free hand and may continue to bat any free ball but they cannot grasp a loose ball with both hands. If the dribbler loses control of the ball, she may regain possession by grasping the ball with both hands. From that point, she can continue to dribble. Players in the maze may not hold or grab the dribbler during the drill. When a player has dribbled the length of the maze from the top of the key to the baseline and returned, she has completed the drill. She then replaces a player on the free throw lane and that player becomes the dribbler.

Coaching Points:

- The dribbler should concentrate on protecting the ball with her body when moving through the maze and grasp the ball with both hands anytime she loses control.

- The drill is designed to teach the dribbler to pick up the ball in traffic rather than continue to bat at a ball that is out of her control.

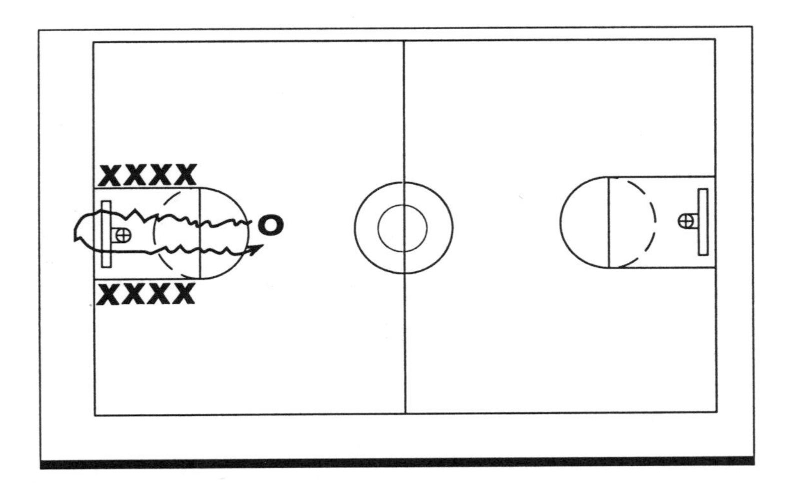

Drill # 3: Scissors Cut

Objective: To improve ball-handling skills and to provide warm up.

Description: Divide the team into four groups and place these groups at the sides of the court with two groups in the guard position and two groups in the forward position. The first person in each of the guard lines should begin with a ball. One player begins the drill in the center of the half court on the free throw line facing one side of the court. The player on the free throw line flashes to one side of the court and receives a pass from the first person in the guard line. The first player in each of the two lines executes a scissors cut off the player on the free throw line with the player who initiated the pass cutting first. The "post" player hands or passes the ball to either of the two cutting players as they pass. The player who receives the pass from the post then passes the ball to the first person in either of the two lines on the opposite side of the court. Both of these players proceed to the end of the line toward which they are cutting. The post player then flashes to the opposite side of the free throw lane and the drill continues. The entrance pass to the post is a pass of some distance; the return pass from the post involves ball handling in close proximity, while the exit pass to the opposite side of the court is also a pass of some distance. Because the drill is continuous it can be used as an early season conditioning drill.

Coaching Point:

- This drill should emphasize both proper passing and receiving techniques.

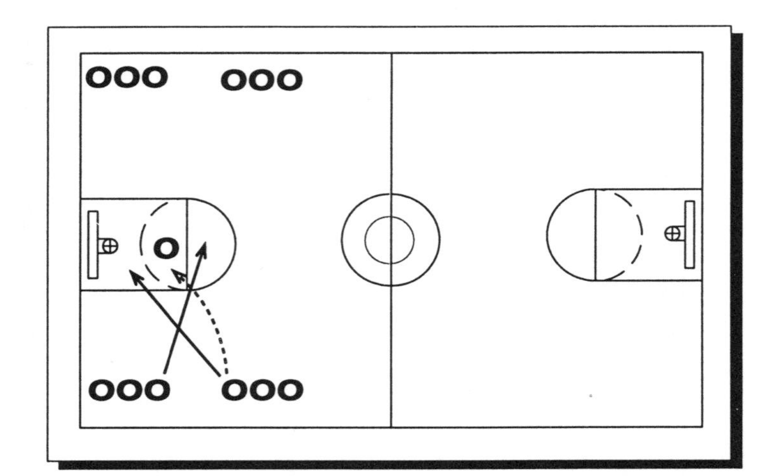

Drill #4: Four Person Dribbling-Pivoting-Passing

Objective: To teach the techniques of dribbling, pivoting and passing.

Description: Divide the team into four groups and position them in the four corners of a half court. The first player in each of the four lines begins the drill with a basketball. The drill begins with the first player in each line dribbling toward the free throw circle. At the circle each player executes a jump stop, a reverse pivot, and a pass to the first person in the line to her immediate left. The players throwing the pass then proceed to the end of the line to which they passed. The players receiving the pass then duplicate the action of the initial group. This drill can be done with or without a basketball, but should be performed with players executing both left and right pivots.

Coaching Points:

- Proper dribbling technique, good jump stops and pivots, and accurate passing should be emphasized.
- The drill is designed to place empahsis on discipline and adherence to patterns.

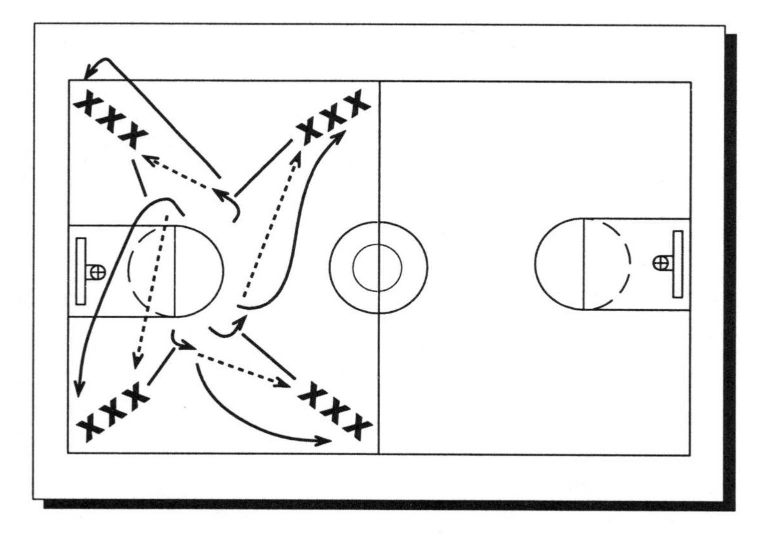

Drill #5: Break and Go

Objective: To improve ball handling, shooting and conditioning.

Description: Position two players at the intersection of the elbows of the lane. A third player serves as the rebounder and is positioned with a basketball in front of the basket on either side. The drill begins with a rebound. As the ball bounces off the backboard the rebounder retrieves it and then outlets the ball to the side closest to her position on the floor. The guard on the side of the rebound breaks to the wing area to receive the pass, while the opposite side guard breaks to the top of the key to receive the second pass coming from the wing area. As a result the ball is centered on the floor and is advanced down the middle of the floor by the player with the ball. The rebounder and the player who received the outlet pass fill their respective sides of the floor and sprint down the floor. The center player advances the ball to the opposite end free throw line and passes to either side player for the lay up.

Coaching Points:

- The rebounder should look upon this as an opportunity to improve the footwork, body position and hand control involved in good rebounding technique.
- The drill should also emphasize accuracy in the outlet and centering passes.

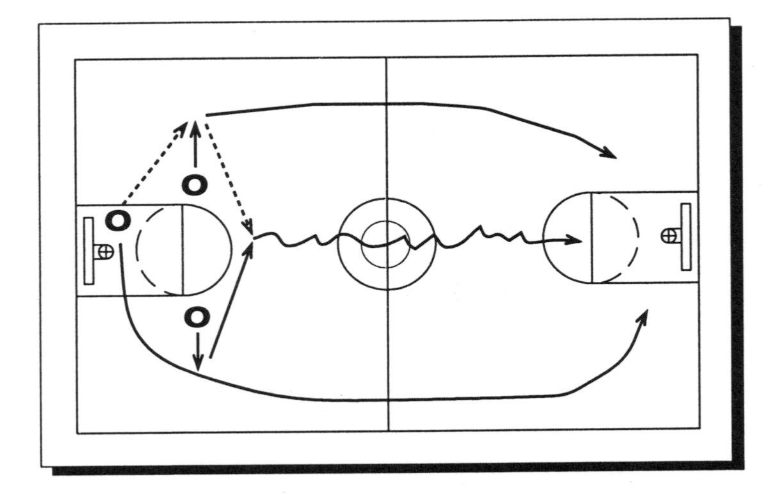

FOOTWORK/ MOVEMENT DRILLS

Drill #6: Toss Out Series

Objective: To teach pivot footwork, dribbling and shooting.

Description: Each individual player begins the drill by standing on the baseline and tossing the ball to a designated spot on the floor. This spot may place her in position to execute a variety of shots: baseline, bank, wing, elbow of the free throw lane, etc. After tossing the ball to the designated spot, the player runs to the ball, catches it and executes one of the following nine moves:

1. pivot, square to the basket, shot;
2. pivot, square up, right hand drive to the basket, lay-up;
3. pivot, square up, left hand drive to the basket, lay-up;
4. pivot, square up, pump fake, right hand drive to the basket, lay-up;
5. pivot, square up, pump fake, left hand drive to the basket, lay-up;
6. pivot, square up, 1 dribble right, jump stop, shot;
7. pivot, square up, 1 dribble left, jump stop, shot;
8. pivot, square up, 2 dribbles right, jump stop, shot;
9. pivot, square up, 2 dribbles left, jump stop, shot.

A player should work both sides of the floor to use both feet in the pivot position.

Coaching Points:

- Catching the ball in a good foot position to execute the initial pivot is critical to the remainder of the drill.

- Being square to the basket before shooting is essential for long-term success in shooting the basketball.

- Becoming comfortable with a number of different options on offense gives the player confidence and more tools to beat the defense. Each of the nine moves has its place in the offensive skills required for effective play and should be learned by each player.

Drill #7: Cut and Dive

Objective: To practice cutting, screening and passing.

Description: This drill involves three players: a guard, a high post and a wing. The players assume their respective positions on one side of the court. The drill begins with the guard passing to the wing and cutting off the high post in such a way as to have to high post player between her and the ball. She proceeds to the area of the low block on the free throw lane. The high post player steps toward the wing and receives a pass. The wing moves to the low block area and screens for the guard. The guard comes off the screen toward the corner, receives the pass, squares herself to the basket and executes a jump shot. The high post rotates to the weak side of the basket for the rebound.

Coaching Points:

- The cutting of the guard by the high post and high post screen are areas where proper execution can make a big difference.
- The areas of preparation leading to the screen and roll are equally as important as the final screen.

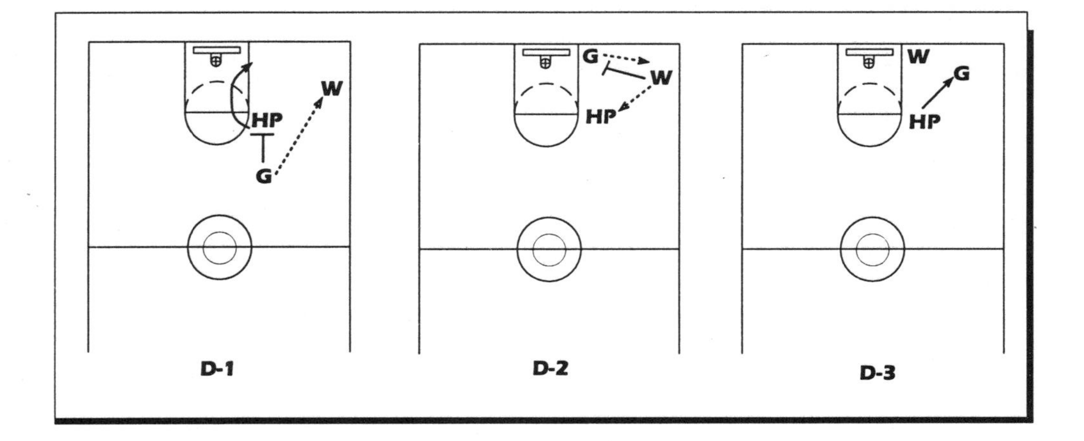

Drill #8: Turn and Face

Objective: To teach the offensive "turn and face" move.

Description: Five defensive players and five offensive players are involved in this drill. Position these players in pairs in the approximate area they would play in your particular offensive set. Each pair of players (defensive players are on the inside) face away from the basket and each offensive player begins the drill with a basketball. The coach calls out the name of a defensive player and that player touches the person she is defending. The offensive player turns and faces the defender. These two players then engage in one-on-one play for the basket. Either the basket is made or the defensive gains possession of the ball.

Coaching Points:

- Learning to "read" the defensive player and determine the best offensive move to basket is the key teaching point of this drill.

- Recognizing how the defender is balanced and what her foot position is can be critical to the success of any offensive player.

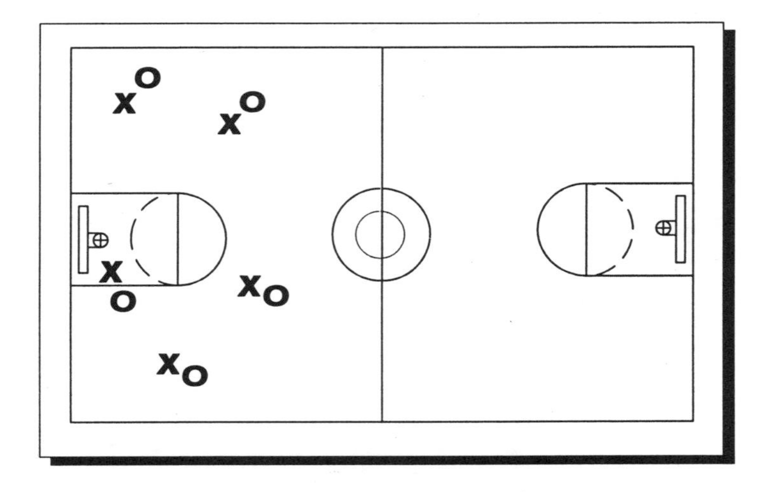

Drill #9: Six Point

Objective: To teach the drop step, slide, denial and open up defensive positions.

Description: Divide the team into two groups and position them in two parallel lines on opposite sides of the division line. Each line should be facing the center of the court. The first person in each line assumes a good defensive position facing the player across the division line. The two players perform the same moves at opposite ends of the court. The initial move is to use the drop step from the starting position to the top of the key. At this point each player uses defensive slides to move laterally to the player's left. At the wing area, the player switches again to the denial position and moves to the lower block on the free throw lane. The stance is again changed to an open up defensive stance and the player slides across the lane to the opposite side. In the final part of the drill the player moves from the lower block of the free throw lane to the opposite wing using a denial defensive stance. The player then rejoins the line at the division line.

Coaching Points:

- Each of the defensive stances should be analyzed for strict adherence to proper technique—low stance, hands ready and in proper position, and quick footwork.
- The emphasis should be on the transitions from one defensive stance to another. How well a player transits from one defensive stance to another can be the difference between success and failure.

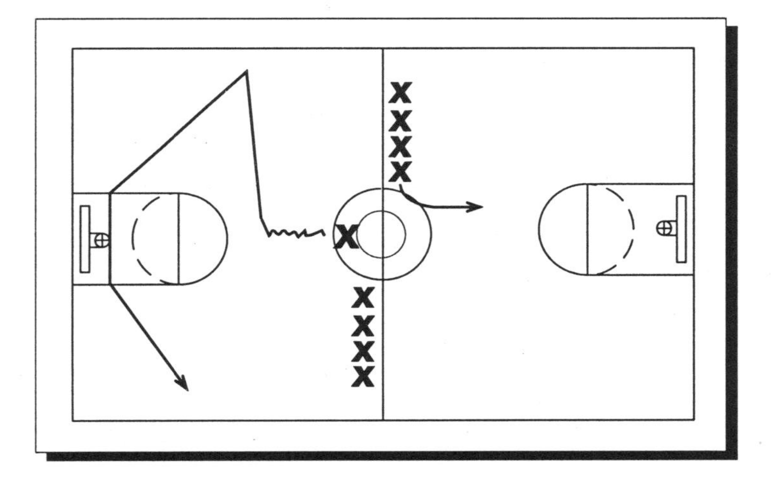

Drill #10 Lane Slide

Objective: To improve defensive foot movement and to teach pursuit angles.

Description: Each player is paired with another. Beginning at either baseline corner of the free throw lane one player (P-1) assumes a defensive position facing the baseline. Her partner (P-2) assumes an offensive position facing the defensive player. Utilizing the sides of the free throw lane as boundaries, the offensive player attempts to dribble toward the free throw line at the opposite end of the free throw lane. The defensive player attempts to turn the offensive player back to the middle of the lane by beating the player to the side boundary of the free throw lane. The drill proceeds until the offensive player crosses the free throw line.

Coaching Points:

- The defensive player should learn to utilize quick foot movements to turn the offensive player away from her desired path.

- The drill should also emphasize that choosing the proper angle of pursuit allows the defensive player to catch up and assume the proper defensive position after being beaten by the offensive player.

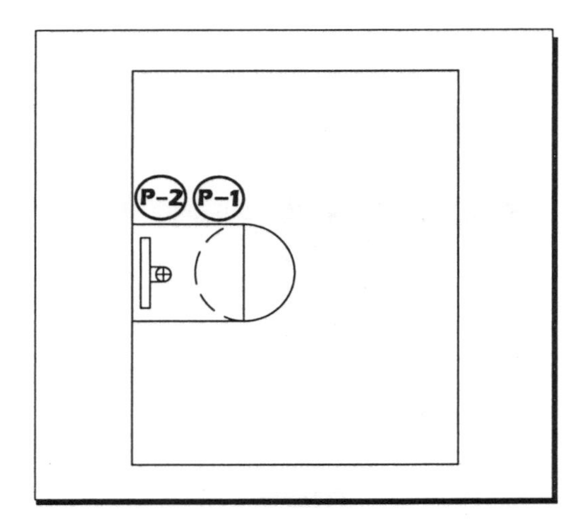

PASSING DRILLS

Drill #11: Pass and Cut

Objective: To improve passing and receiving of the basketball on the move.

Description: Players line up in the four corners of a square area approximately twenty feet square. Multiple number of players may be in each line. The first player in one line passes the ball to the first person in the line to her immediate right and then cuts diagonally across the square. At the mid-point of the square, the player receives a return pass from the person who received the initial pass. The cutting player then passes the ball to the first person in the line toward which she is cutting and goes to the end of that line. The first player to receive the initial pass then cuts diagonally across the square and receives a pass near the mid-point of the square and passes the ball to the first person in the line toward which she is cutting. The process is continued around the square with each person passing, receiving and moving to the end of the line toward which they are cutting.

Coaching Points:

- Executing a good initial pass that the receiver can handle easily should be the first concern during this drill.
- This drill can also be used to enhance foot speed and develop conditioning depending on the intensity level under which the drill is conducted.

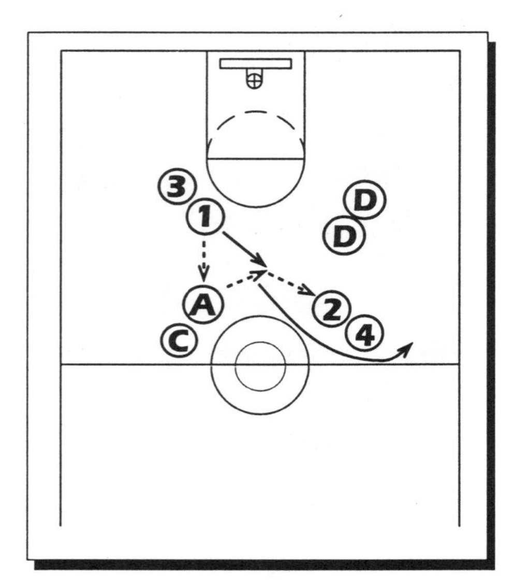

Drill #12: Diamond Passing

Objective: To practice passing and receiving of the ball.

Description: Divide the team into four equal groups and position them at the corners of a square approximately twenty feet apart. Select a corner for the starting point of the drill. The first person in this line and the first person in the line to this player's immediate left should each start with a basketball. These two players start their respective movement simultaneously. Each player passes the ball to the first person diagonally across the square and then follows the pass along the right side of the direction of the pass. Subsequently, she assumes her position at the end of the line to which she passed the ball. The player who received the pass from the starting point then passes the ball to the first person in the line to her immediate right, follows the pass, and assumes her position at the end of the line. The player who received the pass from the player in the line to the immediate left of the starting point passes the ball to the first person in the line to her immediate left. She then follows her pass and assumes a position at the end of the line to which she passed. The balls and players travel around the square in such a manner as to create an "X" with connecting lines between two of the sides.

Coaching Points:

- Making good passes and handling the ball should be emphasized during this drill.
- The drill also instills in the players a sense of discipline and organization, which helps them make the transition to a patterned offense or defense.

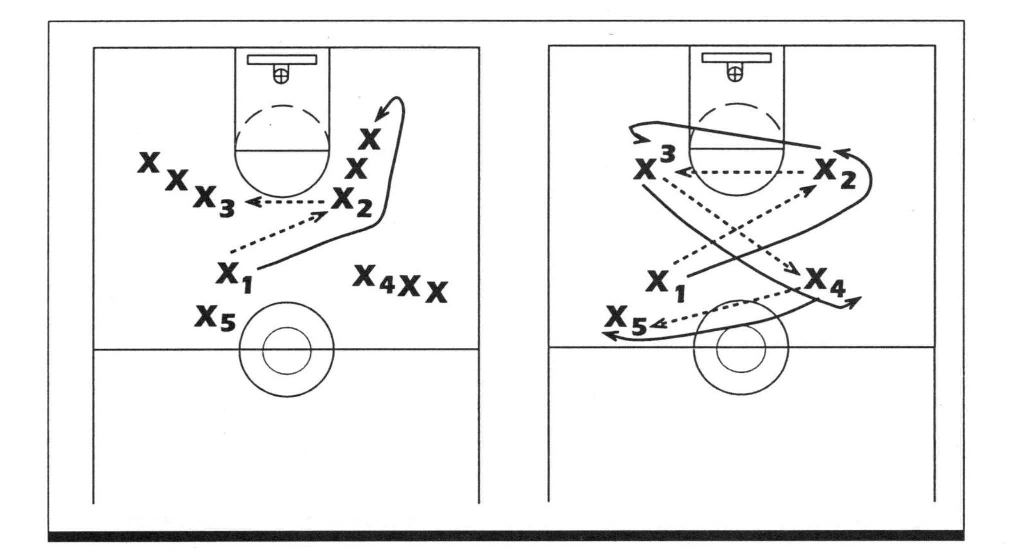

Drill #13: Pass and Catch

Objective: To teach passing, catching, dribbling and shooting.

Description: The team should be divided into three groups of players. The first group consists of four players positioned approximately half way between the center of the court and the appropriate sideline in the area of the top of each free throw circle. These positions can vary slightly from end to end. One half of the remaining players are positioned on the baseline directly outside the free throw lane in a single file line. The remaining half of the team is positioned at the corresponding location on the opposite end of the court. Two balls are required for this drill. The first player in each of the lines on the baseline starts the drill by passing to the player on her side of the court. The passer sprints up the court between the receiver and the sideline. She receives a return pass and dribbles the ball to the half-court line. She then passes to the second player on her side of the court. A sprint between the receiver and the sideline, a return pass, and a lay-up complete the individual's portion of the drill. The player shooting the lay-up rebounds the basketball and passes it to the first person in the line waiting on the baseline. This player passer begins the drill down the opposite side of the court, while the shooter goes to the end of the line. The drill should be conducted continuously until an arbitrary number (e.g., 75) of lay-ups is made by each group.

Coaching Points:

- Accuracy in passing and catching the ball while on the run should be stressed in this drill.
- Moving the ball from the catch to the dribble should also be emphasized.

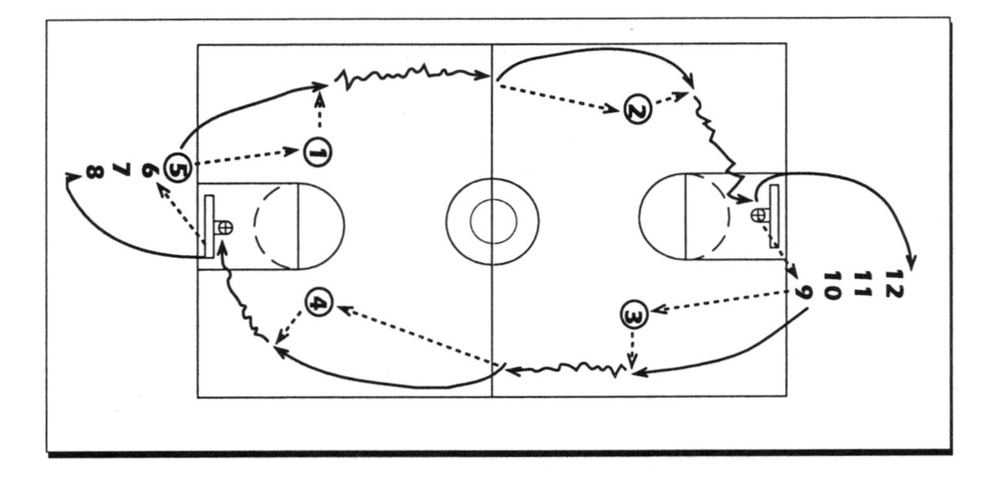

Drill #14: Air It Out

Objective: To teach passing, catching, dribbling and shooting; conditioning

Description: Divide the team into two equal groups. Position one group under the basket outside of the free throw lane and the second group out of bounds in the area. The group under the basket should have at least two basketballs. The first person in the baseline group tosses the ball off the backboard, rebounds the ball and passes it to the first person from the sideline group in the wing position on the court. This player dribbles the length of the court and executes a lay-up. The original rebounder follows the play, rebounds the made lay-up and takes the ball out of bounds. The shooter, after having made the lay-up, breaks to the opposite wing and runs long and wide down the sideline. The pass is made directly from out of bounds to the player running down the sideline. The cutter receives the pass and executes a lay-up with the passer following the play to rebound the made shot. The next pair of players begins their turn when the first lay-up is made at the opposite end of the court. The ball is passed to the next person in the baseline group and the two players involved in the drill switch lines.

Coaching Points:

- For players to throw a long pass with accuracy, proper technique for the release of the pass and the methods to control the spin of the ball should be emphasized.
- To use the drill for conditioning, it should be performed for a minimum of five minutes with a goal of 70 made lay-ups for the entire team.

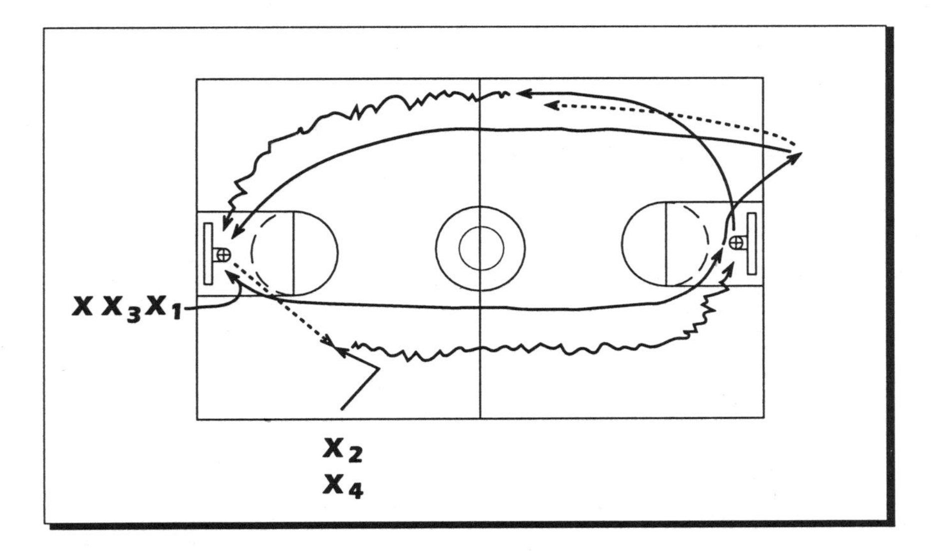

Drill #15: Four-Corner Passing

Objective: To teach passing while on the move; to practice pattern discipline.

Description: In this drill, horizontally refers to passes that go across the court from one sideline toward the other sideline. Vertically refers to passes that go the same direction as the length of the court from baseline to baseline. Divide the players into four equal groups and position them at the four corners of the free throw lane, but not closer to the baseline than the plane of the backboard. The first person in line at two of the corners of the square diagonally opposed to each other has a basketball. These two players begin the drill by passing horizontally to the first person in the line opposite their line. The receivers return the pass as the original passer is moving toward them. The original passer receives the pass and proceeds to hand the ball off to the original receiver. Both first passers then assume a position at the end of the line to which they handed the ball. The second pass the players turn to face the opposite end of the free throw lane. The passer now passes the basketball vertically to the first person in the line and the process is repeated until all the players have moved around the square.

Coaching Points:

- Maintaining the discipline of the drill while executing good passes and handoffs should be the major points of emphasis of this drill. The drill is designed to provide players with the opportunity to practice concentrating on the pattern of the drill, while still executing highly effective, accurate passes.

- Additional balls can be incorporated into the drill to increase the level of difficulty of the drill.

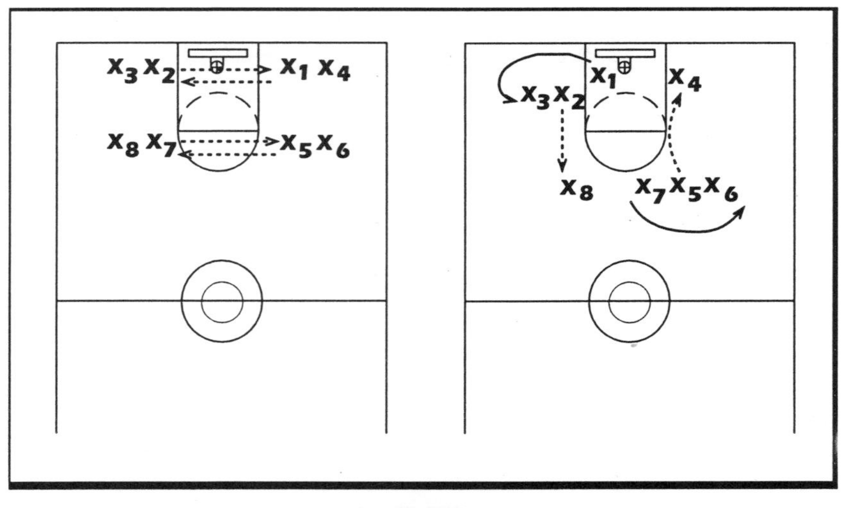

SHOOTING DRILLS

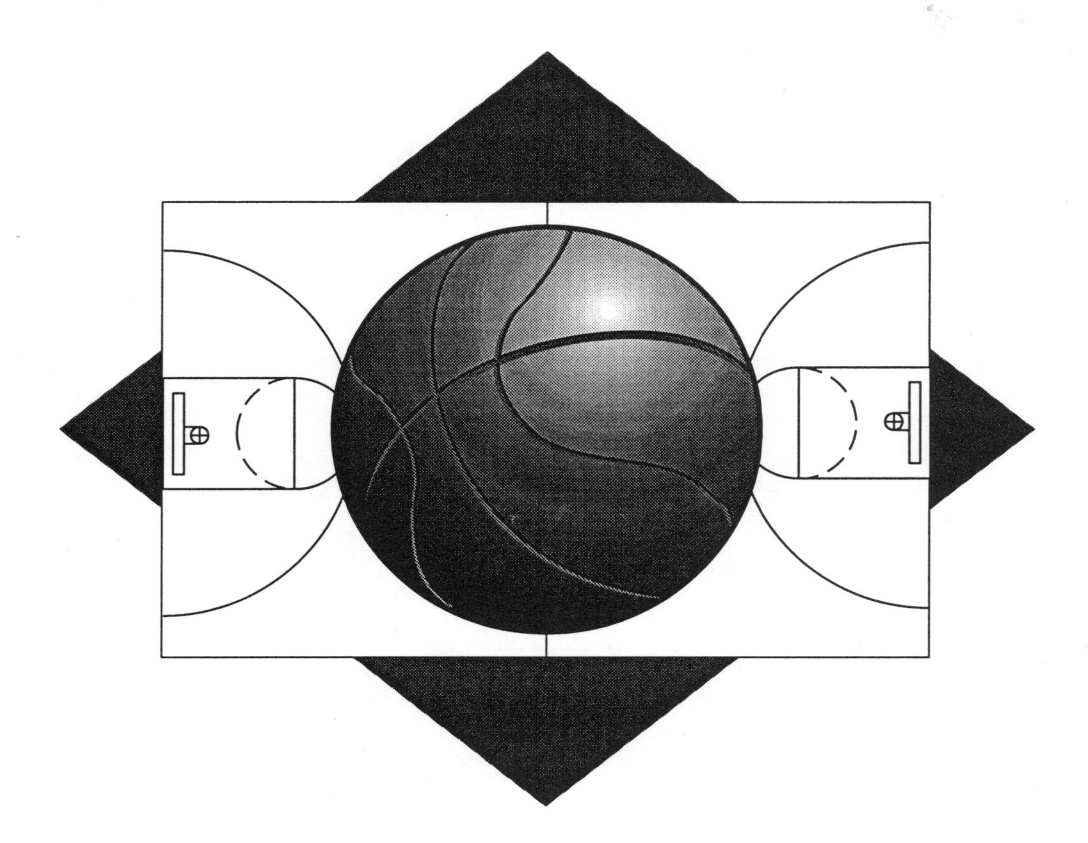

Drill #16: Two Ball Shooting

Objective: To develop proper shooting techniques; to improve concentration.

Description: Four players are needed for this drill. One player serves as the rebounder and the other three players are positioned across the free throw line extended with a player on each wing and the shooter on the free throw line. Each of the wing players begins the drill with a basketball. The shooting player moves across the free throw line to one side and receives a pass, squares to the basket and shoots a jump shot from the intersection of the free throw line and side line of the free throw lane. The shooting player then slides across the free throw lane to the opposite side and shoots from that side. After each shot, the rebounder recovers the ball and returns it to the passer on the wing. This drill should be run for a time varying from 30 seconds to one minute for each shooting player.

Coaching Points:

- A primary teaching point that should be emphasized is that proper shooting technique involves receiving of the pass and squaring to the basket prior to shooting.

- Any focus on quickness should be secondary to receiving the pass and squaring to the basket prior to shooting.

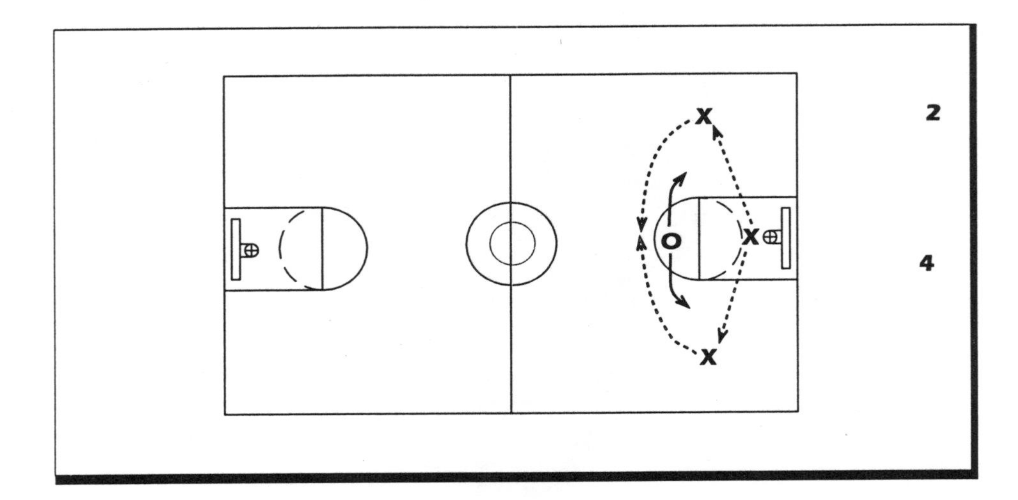

Drill #17: Golf

Objective: To add variety to practicing shooting.

Description: Nine spots are identified on the floor according to the diagram. These spots serve as the "tees" from which the players shoot. Four players compete against each other in this drill. Each player must make a shot from each of the nine spots. All attempts count as one stroke and the player with the fewest shots upon completing the course is declared the winner. A perfect score would be nine shots.

Coaching Points:

- This drill adds variety to practicing shooting by having players take shots from areas with which they may be unfamiliar.
- The coach can introduce additional variety by requiring that each shot must include a fake and drive, a head fake, etc.
- This drill can also be used to help players to concentrate on proper shooting techniques.

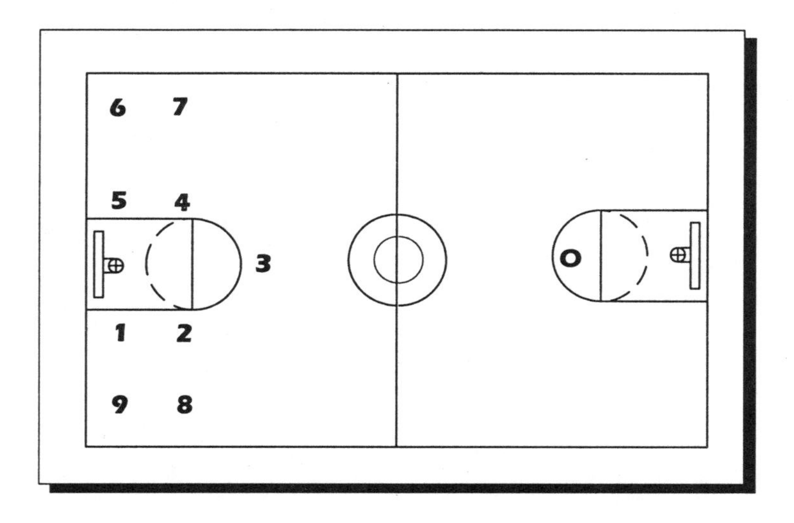

Drill #18: Dribble Spot Shooting

Objective: To practice shooting off the dribble.

Description: One of the best moves for an offensive player is to shoot off the dribble. Position the players in a single line at the division line facing the basket. Nine spots are identified on the floor from which shots may be taken: free throw line, right and left wings, right and left elbows of the free throw lane, right and left bank shots, and right and left baseline. Each player begins the drill by dribbling to one of the designated spots. She executes a good jump stop off the dribble and shoots a jump shot. The following five options are available to each offensive player:

- dribble to the spot, jump stop, shot;
- dribble, crossover at the free throw line, jump stop, shot;
- dribble, crossover at the free throw line, lay-up;
- dribble, hesitation at the top of the key, jump stop, shot;
- dribble, hesitation at the top of the key, lay-up.

Coaching Points:

- The jump stop to gain proper balance and power for the jump shot is critical for success.

- A player's motion from the stop of her dribble to the execution of the jump shot should be quick and fluid; since any hesitation in this action may allow the defense time to recover and possibly block the shot.

- Remind the players of the three-point line and to follow all shots.

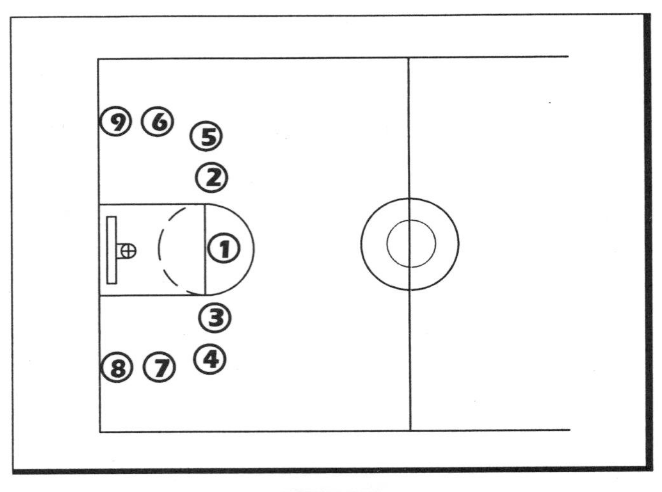

Drill #19: Around the World

Objective: To teach and practice proper shooting techniques; conditioning.

Description: Five spots on the floor are selected for each drill. These spots may vary from position to position based upon which player is participating in the drill. The shooting spots should start on one baseline and work around the half court in an arc to the opposite side of the court with shots being taken from both corner, both wings and the center of the half court. Players in this drill participate alone. Each player takes a shot, rebounds the shot runs to the next spot. Each player should go "around the world" an arbitrary number of times (e.g. five) with the goal being to make all of the shots taken.

Coaching Points:

- Proper squaring of the shoulders, foot placement and hand/wrist action should be consistent and repetitive. Shooting a basketball effectively is a skill that is best learned through duplicating proper techniques.

- Fatigue and lack of motivation are two of the biggest inhibitors to learning proper shooting technique.

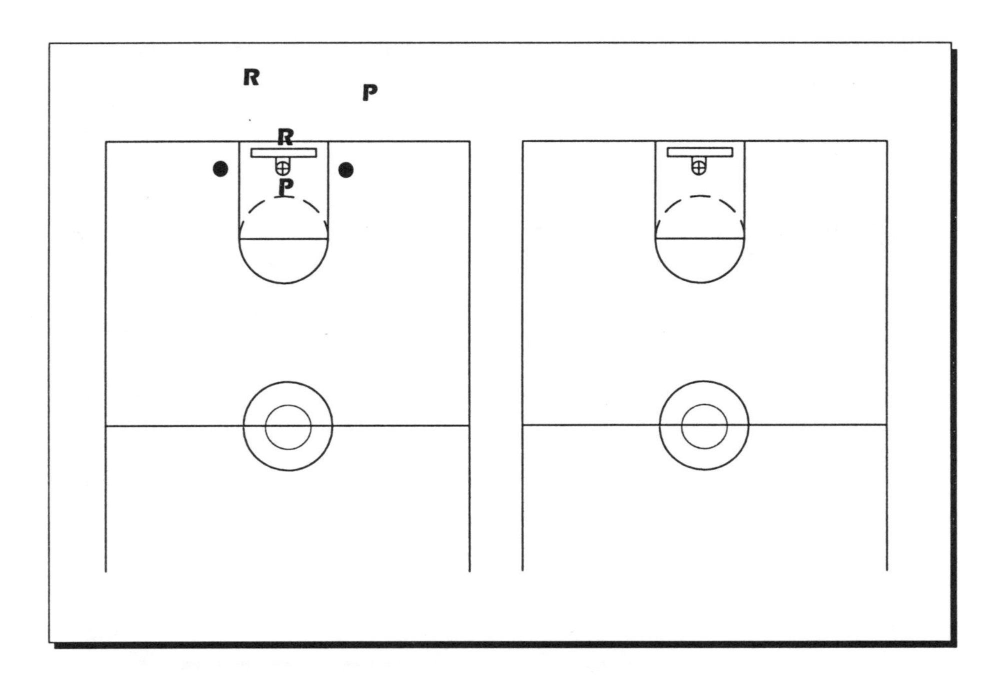

Drill #20: Chase and Shoot

Objective: To practice recovering loose balls and shooting off the recovery.

Description: Place one basketball on either side of the free throw lane (outside the lane) approximately one half the distance between the free throw line and the baseline. Position the offensive player in the middle of the lane approximately three feet from the free throw line facing the free throw line. A rebounding player is placed directly under the basket. Begin the drill by having the shooting player turn and recover either one of the balls on the floor, square herself to the basket and execute a jump shot. After the first ball is shot, the offensive player recovers the second ball and again shoots a short jump shot. The rebounder rebounds each of the shots and re-positions the balls back to their original spots on the floor. Each player spends thirty seconds as either the shooter or the rebounder and then switches roles.

Coaching Points:

- Finding the loose ball on the floor and reacting to the location are keys to the recovery.
- Altering the placement of the ball on the floor from time to time can help the player learn to locate the ball more quickly.
- Following the recovery of the ball, the player must be prepared to quickly shoot the basketball before the defense can apply any pressure to her.

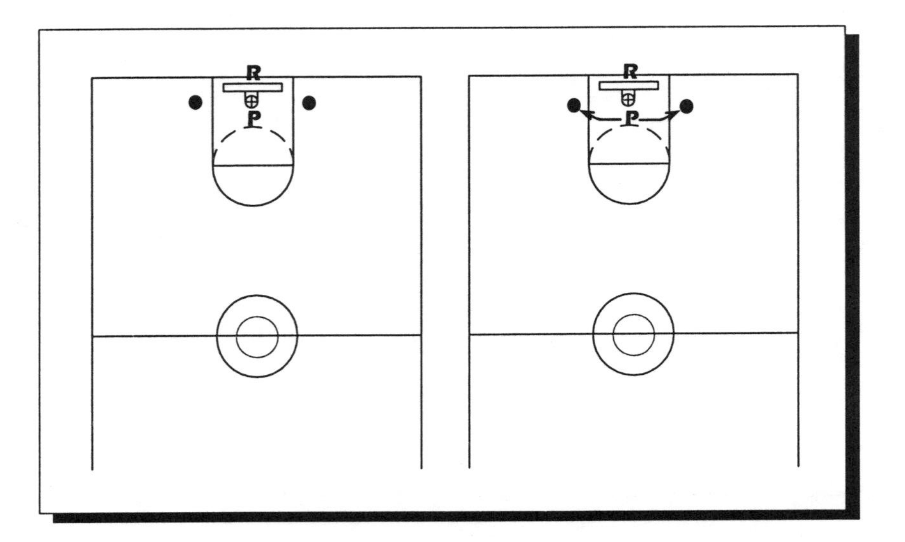

Drill #21: Rushin' Lay-ups

Objective: To practice shooting lay-ups; conditioning

Description: Divide the team into two equal groups positioned at the elbow. To start the drill, the player at the front of the line on the right dribbles to the basket and shoots a right handed lay-up. The first person in the opposite line rebounds the ball and passes it to the first person in the shooting line. Both the rebounder and the shooter then sprint the length of the court switching sides from their respective starting points and assume the same positions at the opposite end of the floor. The drill proceeds until all players have shot a right handed lay-up at one end of the floor and have moved to the other end. The final rebounder at one end of the floor dribbles down the floor and passes to the first person in the shooting line at the opposite end. The drill is then repeated using left handed lay-ups.

Coaching Points:

- While this drill is primarily a conditioning drill, the teaching of good shooting form including footwork should not be overlooked.
- The drill is also used to teach both right and left handed shooting by switching the sides from which the shots are taken.

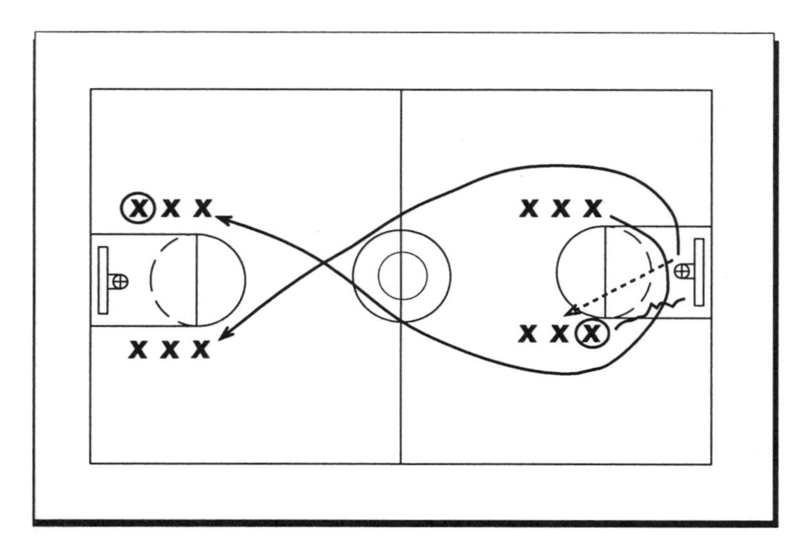

Drill #22: Circle Shooting

Objective: To practice shooting at the end of the fast break; to improve ball-handling skills; conditioning.

Description: Every player begins the drill with a basketball. Divide the team into two groups and position the groups in two lines with the first person in each line approximately half way between the top of the free throw circle and the sideline to their right. The line should face the basket and be formed behind the first person toward the division line of the court. In succession, each player dribbles to the mid-post area. She executes a bank jump shot, rebounds the shot and dribbles to the end of the opposite line. The drill continues with the players continuously dribbling in a counter-clockwise circle shooting at both ends of the court. After two-three minutes, the direction is reversed. Locations of the shots can be changed from bank shot to the elbow of the free throw lane, lay up, 15-foot wing jump shot, eight-foot baseline shot, etc. The dribble can also be changed from straight line to crossover dribble, behind the back or between the legs.

Coaching Points:

- The drill can be altered to create various situations that evolve from the fast break—three-on- two, two-on-two, two-on-one, etc.
- The drill also provides players with an opportunity to improve upon their ball-handling skills.
- Some conditioning can be provided by the drill depending upon the duration and the level of intensity of the drill.

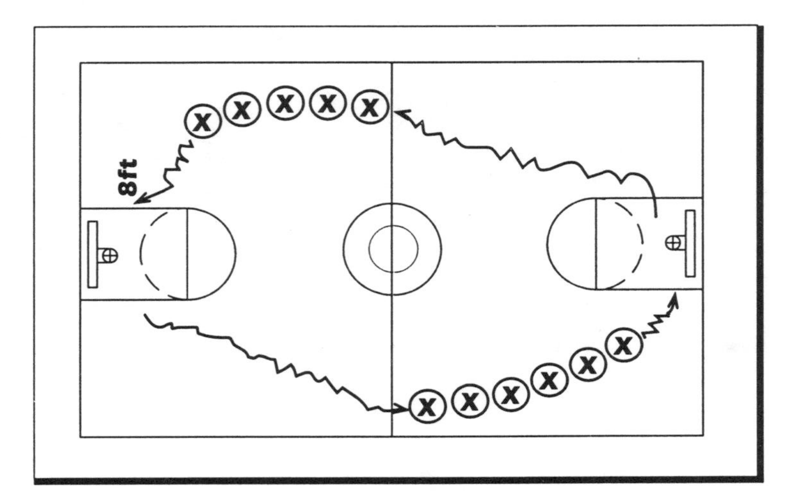

Drill #23: 25-Shot Shoot-Out

Objective: To practice shooting under a variety of conditions; conditioning.

Description: This drill involves two players—one player in a rebounding position near the basket and one player on the free throw line facing the basket. The player on the free throw line takes twenty-five (25) shots according to the following schedule: ten (10) jump shots without dribbling the ball prior to shooting; five (5) jump shots utilizing one dribble of the basketball moving to either side from the original position; five (5) jump shots utilizing more than one dribble of the basketball to either side of the original position; and five (5) "anything goes" jump shots that allow the player to develop unique moves. After each shot, the player must return to the original position in the center of the free throw line. The shooter must make at least 13 of the 25 shots each drill.

Coaching Points:

- Emphasis should be placed on squaring the shoulders to the basket after receiving a pass or moving from one position to another on the floor and develop a good, quick first step to free themselves for an open shot.
- Having players in constant motion also provides a conditioning aspect to the drill.
- While the shots are not exceptionally long range, the requirement that a player must make over 50 percent of her shots does add a demonstrable degree of difficulty.

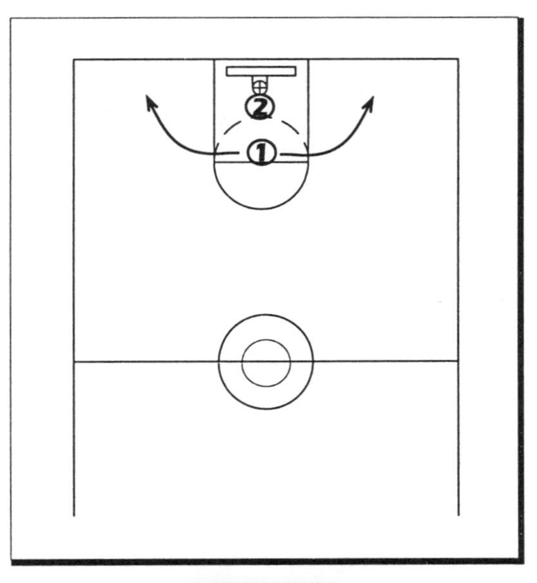

Drill #24: Pressure Shooting

Objective: To improve jump shooting and foul shooting under pressure.

Description: Divide the players into two equally sized groups. The teams line up on the baseline on either side of the basket approximately half way between the sideline and the basket facing the court. The first player in each line should be on the baseline. While using the outside hand, the first player dribbles to half court, executes a crossover dribble to the opposite hand and takes a jump shot from the free throw line. If the shot is missed, the player must rebound the basketball and return to the foul line to shoot a free throw. Each player must make a basket—either a jump shot or a free throw. The player then returns to the opposite end of the court by dribbling to half court with the outside hand and executing a crossover dribble to the opposite hand. She then takes a jump shot from the free throw line. Again at this end, the player must either make a jump shot or a free throw similar to the situation at the first end of the court. Following a made basket, the ball is passed to the next person in line. The first team to have each player make a basket is the winner.

Coaching Points:

- Working on the jump shot off the dribble is the major skill to develop. Shooting free throws under the pressure of the competition is also an essential teaching point.

- The drill can help develop foot speed and improve conditioning by having the players participate at full speed and full court.

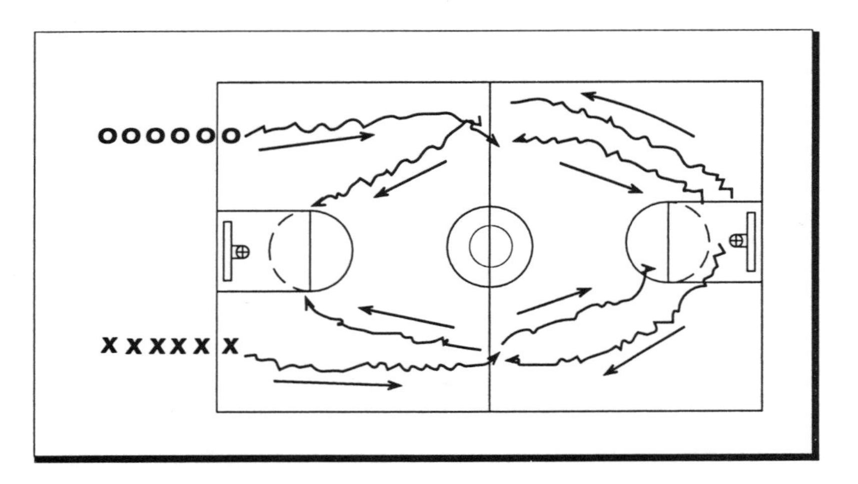

Drill #25: Chair Obstacle Shooting

Objective: To practice dribbling and shooting while maintaining balance and speed.

Description: Three chairs are placed on the court—one chair at the head of the key and another on either side of the free throw line extended approximately three feet outside the free throw lane. The player starts with the ball at the chair located at the head of key. She dribbles the ball with her outside hand to either of the chairs on the side and shoots from that position. The player then rebounds the shot and dribbles with her outside hand around the middle to the opposite side chair and shoots again. The process is repeated for one minute. Score can be kept to establish competition between players.

Coaching Points:

- Controlling the ball under full speed conditions around the obstacles should be stressed. Each shot should be taken under controlled conditions from the speed dribble.

- Good foot positioning and squaring the shoulders to the basket prior to the shot should be emphasized.

- Players should practice dribbling with both hands and shooting from both sides of the floor.

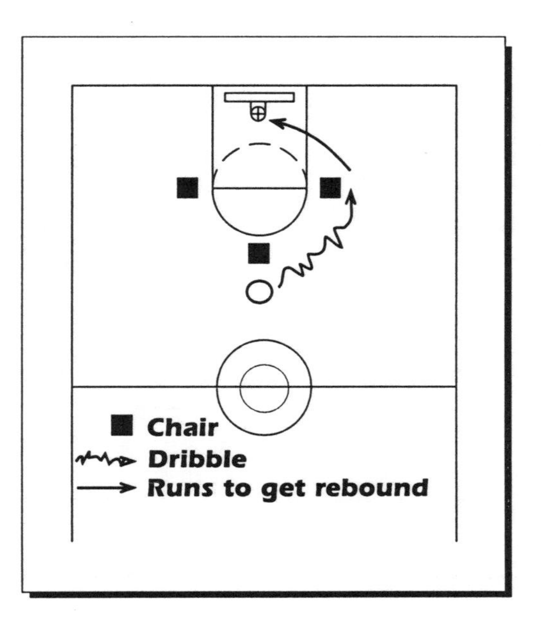

Drill #26: Shoot and Follow

Objective: To improve shooting and the ability to follow a shot.

Description: Position four players in the following sequence—one player directly under the basket with a ball in her hand, the other three players spread in an arc around the half court approximately 15-20 feet from the basket. The drill begins with the player under the basket passing the ball to any of the three other players. These players must be in motion to receive the pass. After passing the ball, the passer closes the distance between the two players and assumes a good defensive stance. The receiver then squares to the basket, shoots a good jump shot and follows her shot for the rebound. The defensive player attempts to screen out the shooter, but cannot rebound the ball. The shooter rebounds the ball and passes to either of the two remaining players. The original passer replaces the original shooter. The drill begins again with a new passer and a new receiver. Each set of four players should continue this drill for 4-5 minutes.

Coaching Points:

- The offensive player and her actions should be making game-like moves before receiving the pass and upon receiving the ball should adhere to sound offensive shooting principles—square her shoulders to the basket, keep the ball up high after receiving the pass, stay balanced on the shot, etc.

- The shooter must concentrate on following her shot for any available rebound.

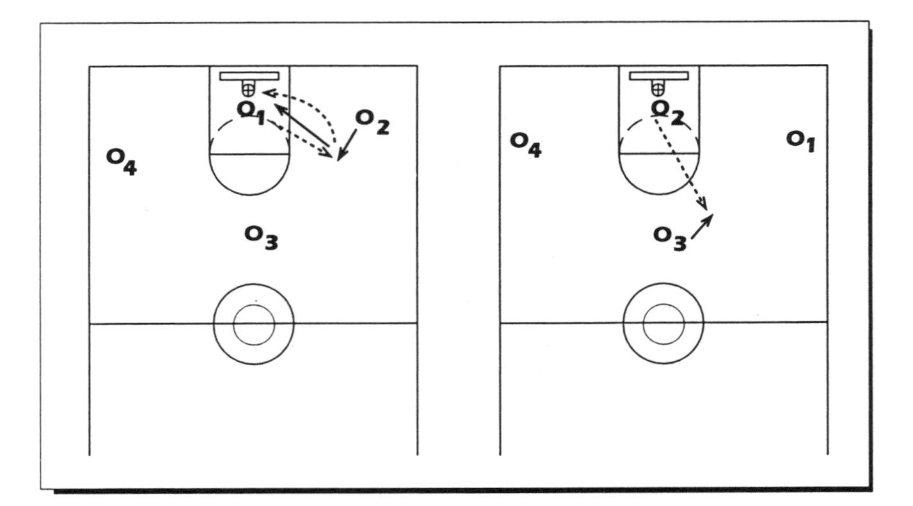

CHAPTER 5

POST PLAY DRILLS

Drill #27: Post-It

Objective: To teach offensive skills for play in the post area.

Description: Position two players just outside the free throw lane. Position two additional players, each with a basketball in the wing positions. The drill begins with a signal to the two post players to switch positions. One player should rotate across the free throw lane by using an arc closer to the free throw line and the other player should use an arc closer to the basket. Each post player should reestablish her position outside the free throw lane just above the blocks. The wing player on her side then throws a bounce pass to the post player. Upon receiving the basketball, the post player can use one of three offensive moves: (1) drop step to the basket; (2) turn, face the basket and shoot the short jump shot; or (3) turn, face the basket, head fake, dribble and shoot a short jump shot or layup.

Coaching Points:

- This drill should emphasize the options available to the post player after she receives the ball. She should perform offensive moves by turning toward the baseline to avoid the defensive congestion of the lane.

- The drill should also be a learning experience for the two players who make the passes from the wings. The wing player should fake or move to a new position using either a dribble or both hands to best simulate game conditions.

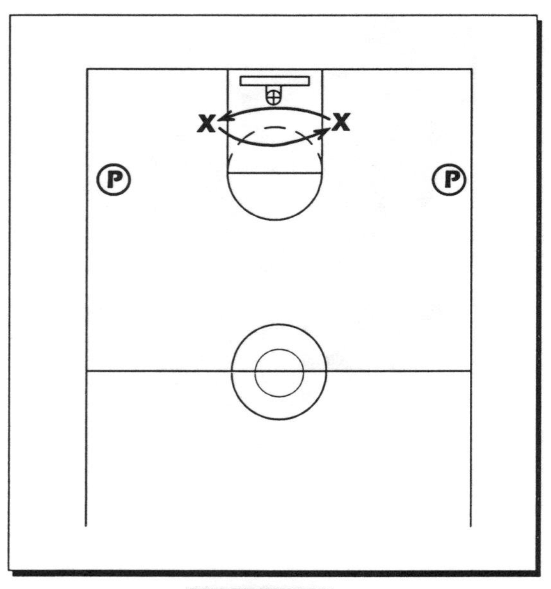

Drill #28: Cool Posting

Objective: To help post players develop poise in a crowd.

Description: Three players who serve as passers in this drill are positioned with one on each wing and one at the top of the key. Each of the players designated as a passer begins the drill with a basketball. A single post player is positioned on either side of the free throw lane. This drill begins with one defensive player and the post player. Eventually, another defensive player is added to provide a double-team situation and then another player to create a triple-team situation. The post player starts the drill by positioning herself to receive a pass from any one of the three passers. After the ball is received in the post area, the offensive player pivots and faces the defense. If the shot is available, she takes it. If the shot is not available, the ball is passed out and the post player moves to another position to receive a second pass and so on. The defensive players can be adjusted to present different situations to the post player. Their actions and movements can be changed periodically to vary the situation (e.g., they may be required not to use their hands, they may be required to bump the offensive player with their body, etc.).

Coaching Points:

- This drill helps the offensive post player become accustomed to different styles of defensive play and the appropriate response to each.

- This drill can be adjusted to give the post player a straight one-on-one look, a collapsing double-team defense, or even a triple-team defense.

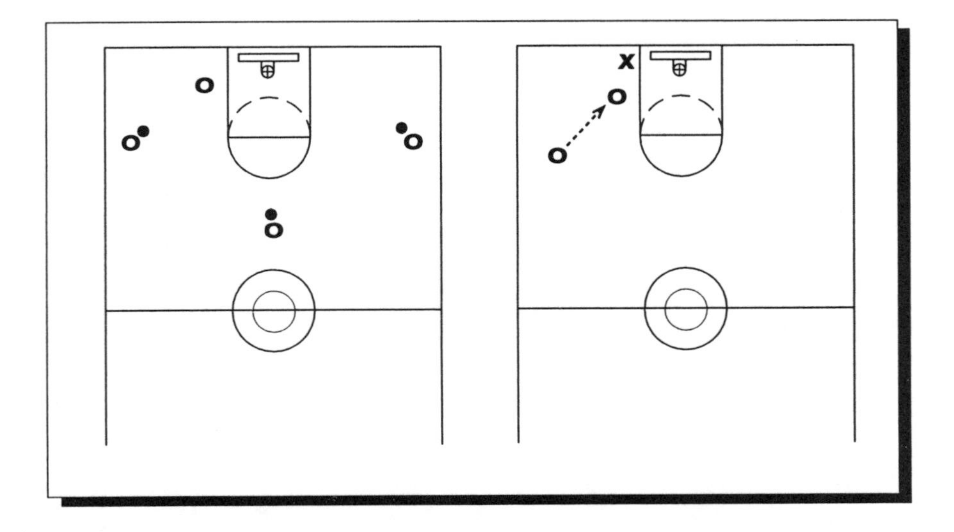

Drill #29: Ball Reaction and Power-up

Objective: To teach players to rebound and to return the ball with strength to the basket.

Description: Initially this drill only involves an offensive post player (0-1) and the coach. The coach takes a position slightly behind the free throw line facing the basket with a basketball in hand. 0-1 positions herself in the midpost area facing the free throw line. The drill begins with the coach throwing the ball off the backboard and 0-1 executing a quick pivot to face the basket. The rebound is made and the player takes one dribble and powers up to the basket using both hands to secure the ball on the way up to the basket. Later, variations of the drill can include requiring the player to the pump fake and/or head fake before going up for the lay up. One or two defensive players (X-1, X-2) may subsequently be added to increase the level of difficulty for the offensive player. The players should be rotated after each attempt when using defensive players.

Coaching Points:

- Both the speed and the angle of the toss from the coach should be varied to give the player a more realistic situation on each rebound.
- The dribble and the step toward the basket should be low, controlled and made with the inside foot to the defensive player in an effort to shield the shot from the defensive player by using her body.

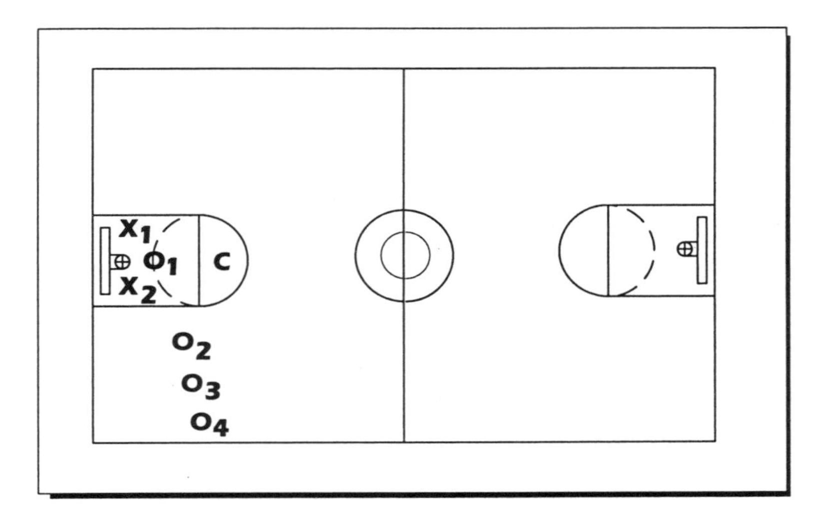

Drill #30: Power Rebound

Objective: To develop balance and the ability to establish a good center of gravity.

Description: A shooting player is positioned at the elbow of the lane. A defensive player assumes a good rebound position in the center of the free throw lane. The coach is positioned between the defensive rebounder and the basket. On the shot, the defensive player rebounds the ball, while the coach applies physical pressure that requires the player to concentrate on establishing balance and a low center of gravity. The degree of contact is controlled by the coach to give the player different types of situations.

Coaching Points:

- This drill should emphasize the importance of maintaining good balance following physical contact.

- The players' footwork while in the air following contact and the ability to land with a good, wide base are essential traits of an effective rebounder.

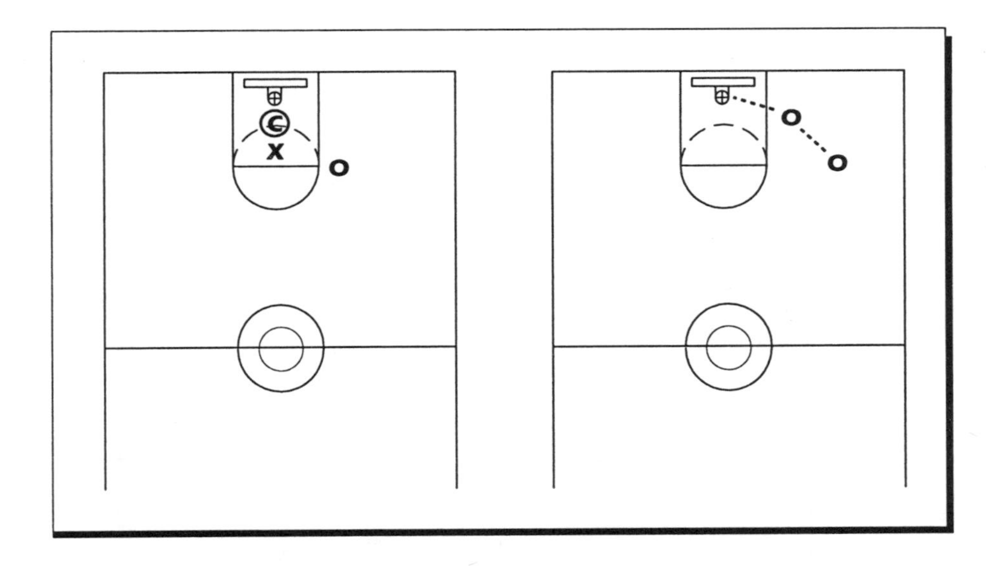

Drill #31: Cutting Loose

Objective: To improve defensive post play.

Description: One offensive (O-1) and one defensive (X-1) player begin the drill in position at the top of the key and in line with the side line of the free throw lane extended. The coach (C) takes a position in the wing area on the same side of the half court as the players. The drill begins with the offensive player passing the ball to the coach and cutting into the post area of the free throw lane in an attempt to receive a return pass from the coach. If the initial pass is defended, the offensive player may make subsequent cuts within the free throw lane in an effort to free herself for a pass from the coach. The defensive player must defend all the possible cuts by the offensive player. Variations of the drill can include weakside help or the absence of weakside help and the adjustments associated with each situation.

Coaching Points:

- The defensive player must decide whether to front the offensive player, play ball side defense, or over-play pressure on the ball side.
- The primary emphasis of this drill should be on maintaining an appropriate position for each specific situation.

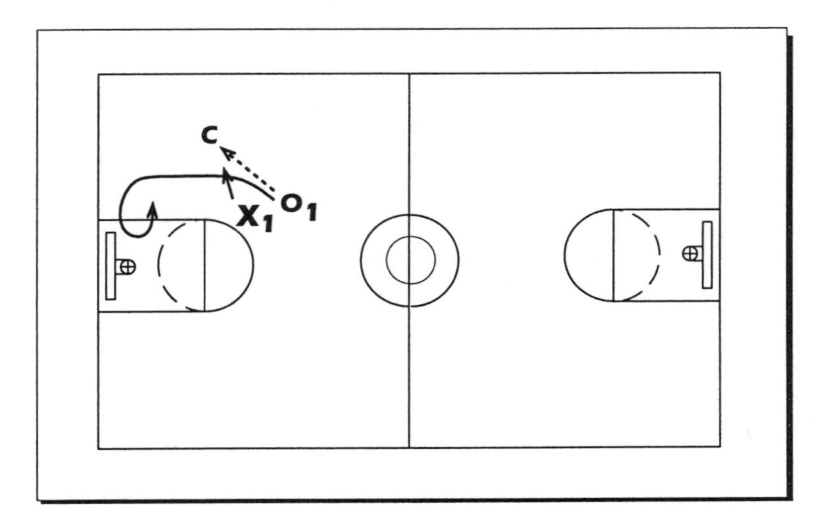

REBOUNDING DRILLS

Drill #32: Four Line Box Out

Objective: To teach proper boxing-out techniques.

Description: Two defensive players are positioned at the baseline corners of the free throw lane, each with a basketball. Two offensive players are positioned at the elbows of the lane. Each defensive player passes the ball to her respective offensive player and follows the pass while maintaining good defensive position. The offensive player catches the ball and shoots from the spot of the pass reception. The defensive player then calls "shot" and boxes out the shooter. After the defense has adjusted to the demands of the initial drill, the offense can be allowed one or two dribbles after the pass. This adds more realism to the drill and helps to prevent the defensive player from using poor footwork since she knows that the offensive player can now drive to the basket.

Coaching Points:

- The defense must follow the pass and assume a proper guarding position as soon as possible after the pass is made. This includes maintaining good foot position to prevent the drive to the basket and contesting the shot by having the left arm up.

- Maintaining contact with the offensive player and keeping her away from the rebound through body position are the key points to boxing out.

- Emphasize should be on achieving a proper body position through footwork, rather than holding with the hands to minimize "lazy" boxing out and the potential for fouls being called for holding.

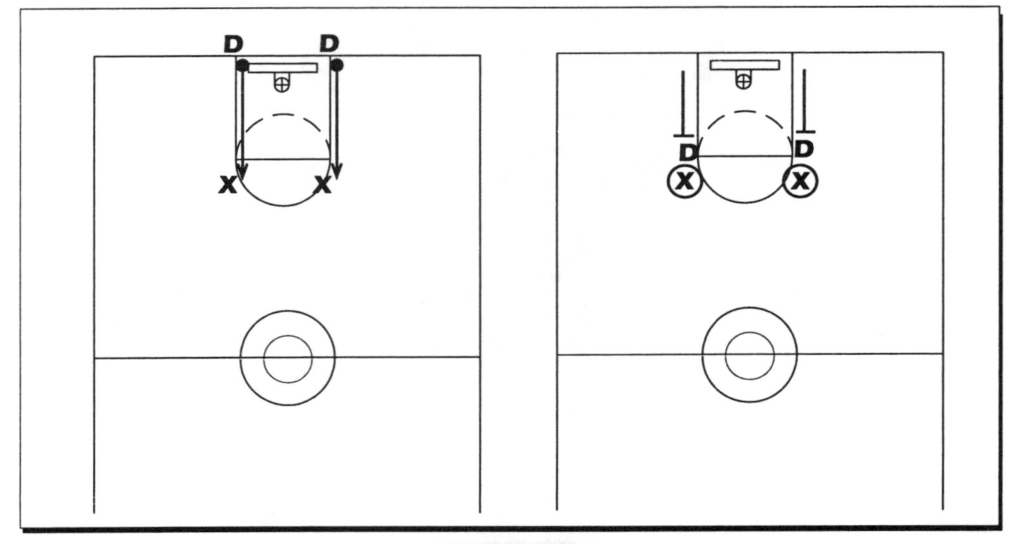

Drill #33: Two Ball Outlet Rebounding

Objective: To teach defensive rebounding and outlet passing.

Description: Two shooting players are positioned with basketballs at the elbows. A third offensive player is in the lane near the basket. Four defensive players are also on the court. One is the defensive rebounder responsible for blocking out the shooter and either getting the rebound in the event of a missed shot or inbounding the ball following a basket. Two players are positioned on either side of the court near the 28-foot mark. The final player is near the opposite basket. Either shooter takes a shot and the defensive player in the lane blocks out the shooter. If the basket is made, the defensive player catches the ball before it hits the floor and inbounds the ball to her teammate near the opposite basket for an uncontested lay-up. If the basket is missed, the defensive player rebounds the ball and outlets it to either of the players located near the 28-foot mark on the floor. The offensive player in the free throw lane pressures the rebounder attempting the outlet pass. After the outlet pass is completed, the other shooter shoots the ball and the drill continues as stated above. The player who received the first outlet pass returns the basketball to the first shooter and so on. Each defensive rebounder stays in the drill for two to three minutes at a time.

Coaching Points:

- This drill should stress good defensive rebounding technique: keeping the arms up, boxing out the shooter without holding or fouling, anticipating where the rebound, and maintaining a body position with a good low base.
- Keeping the outlet pass from being intercepted and passing the ball in a manner that assists the receiver in moving the ball up the floor should be emphasized.

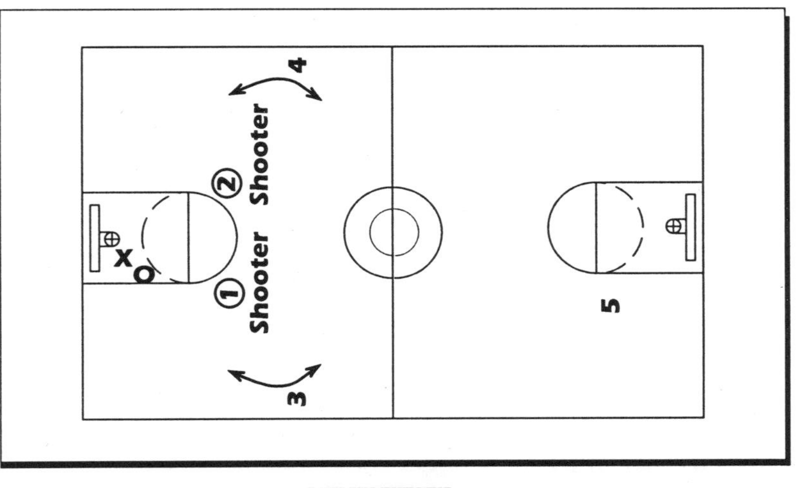

Drill #34: Box and Trap

Objective: To teach blocking out on the rebound and the basics of the 2-2-1 press.

Description: The coach is the only shooter in this drill unless the offense can score on a lay-up. Position the four defensive players (X-1, X-2, X-3, X-4) at the four corners of the free throw lane. Three offensive players (O-1, O-2, O-3) are positioned anywhere on the court and may move around and pass the ball during the drill. The ball is passed around until the shot is taken by the coach. All defensive players then box out the offensive player(s) in their area and rebound the missed shot. If the offense rebounds the ball and scores, the drill begins again with the coach having the ball. If the defense rebounds the ball they go into transition down the court and play 4 on 3 until they score or lose the ball. Upon scoring at the other end, the four players are on defense again and set up the front four positions in the traditional 2-2-1 press. The three offensive players inbound the ball the baseline and the ball and the ball advances up the floor with the four defensive players trapping at every opportunity. The three offensive players advance the ball and play 3 on 4 until they score or lose the ball.

Coaching Points:

- This drill should stress to the defense the importance of locating offensive players and boxing them out immediately after the shot.
- The second half of the drill should emphasize good foot position and the avoidance of reaching with hands during the trap.

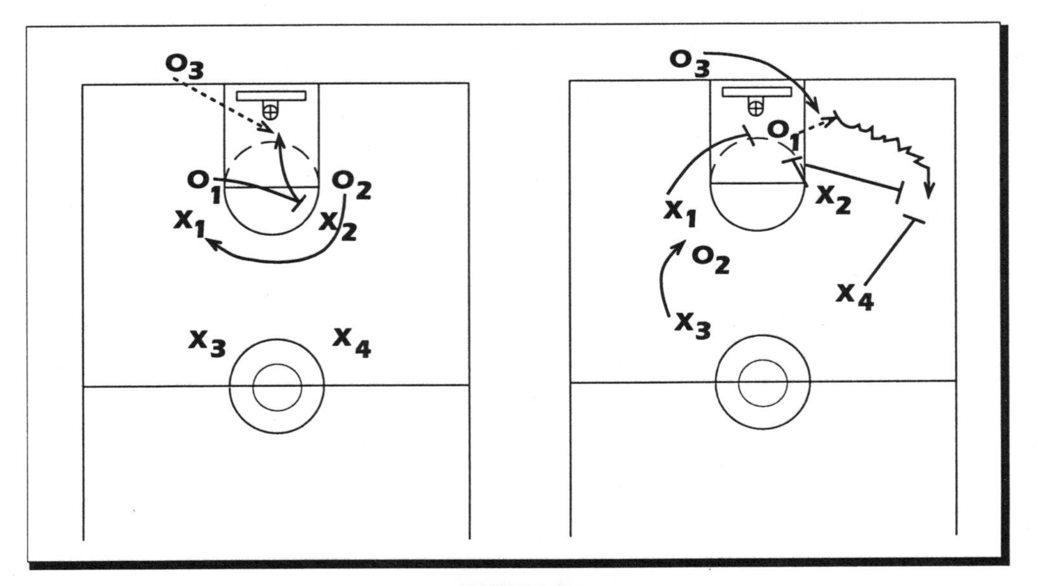

Drill #35: React and Move

Objective: To properly react to the position of the basketball when rebounding.

Description: Randomly place cones in the free throw lane to serve as obstacles for the players to go around. The players form a single line on the free throw line. A rebounding ring is suggested. The coach shoots and the first player in line avoiding the cones moves to retrieve the rebound. The player must rebound the ball before it hits the floor and then outlet the ball to the closest wing. Changing the location from which the shots are taken will add reality to the drill. Changing the arrangement of the cones will accustom the players to different situations and choosing alternate routes to the rebound.

Coaching Point:

- Learning to react to those rebounds that do not come off the rim as anticipated can provide an advantage for the player and enable her to earn extra rebounds each game.

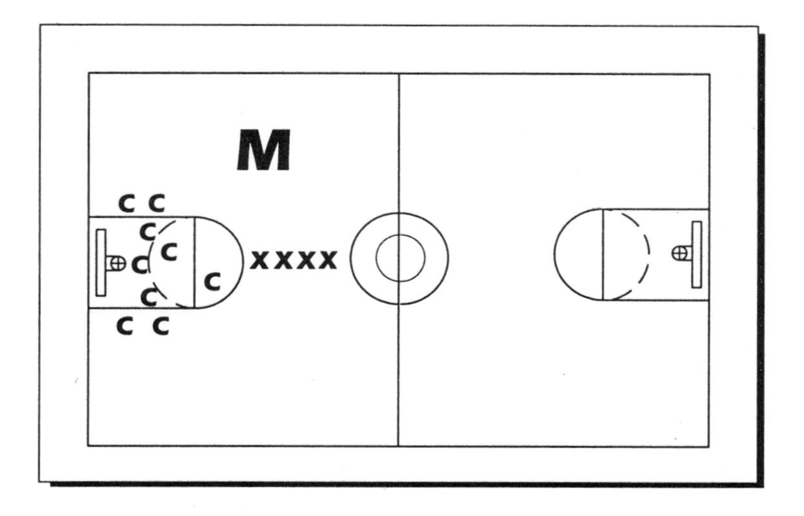

Drill #36: Pressure Cooker

Objective: To teach rebounding when applying full-court pressure defense.

Description: Four offensive players line up along one side line, equally spaced from approximately ten feet inside one baseline to ten feet inside the opposite baseline. The first player in line begins the drill with a basketball. At the top of the key at the end where the ball is when the drill begins, two defensive players are positioned facing the side line where the players are lined up. The drill begins with the four players passing (no dribbling allowed) the ball down the court. The two defensive players retreat down the court as the ball is being passed. The final person in the passing line takes a shot from her position on the floor and follows the shot to the basket. The second-to-last person follows the shot in an attempt to rebound the missed attempt. The two defensive players locate the offensive players and block them out. If the defenders rebound the ball, they are rotated out of the drill. On the other hand, if the offensive players rebound the ball, they are rotated out of the drill, while the defensive players must go again.

Coaching Points:

- The defensive players may not leave their positions until the initial pass is made. This simulates the breaking of the press by the offense and minimizes the ability of the defenders to get much of a jump in getting down the court.

- The block out should include direct contact between the defensive player and her offensive counterpart.

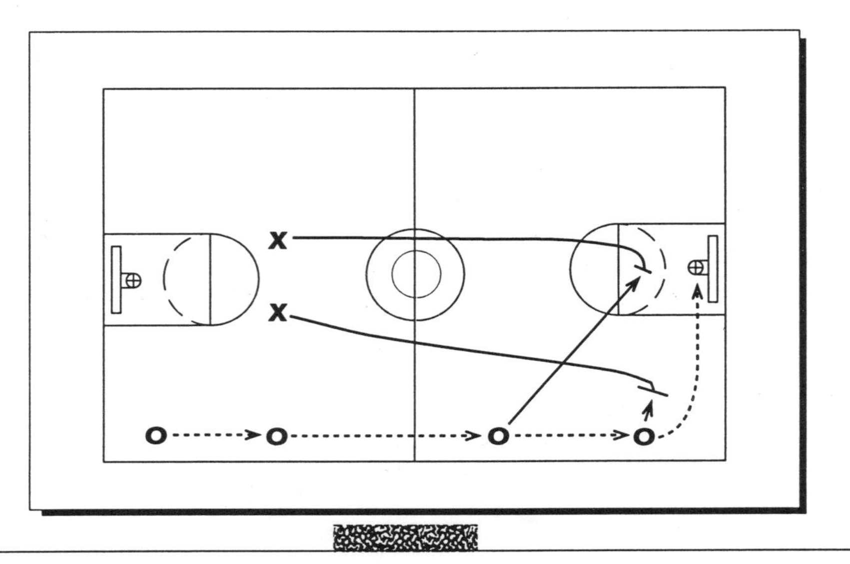

Drill #37: Triangle Drill

Objective: To teach the basic rebounding triangle.

Description: This is a five-on-five drill. Position the five offensive players around the half court in any typical offensive set. The defensive players should be playing loose defense but must always be close enough to the player they are guarding to ensure the ability to establish contact in the event of a shot. All the defensive players are instructed to use a pivot into the offensive player to box out. The defensive rebound is outletted to the wing area to simulate the beginning of the fast break. The addition of an offensive weave to make the defense slide through the screens can introduce variety to this drill.

Coaching Point:

- The pivot made by the defensive player may be made in either direction depending upon the location of the offensive player to be boxed out. The box out should include and concentrate on the timing to establish contact, the bending of the back, and finally, the legal use of the elbows to maintain the position desired.

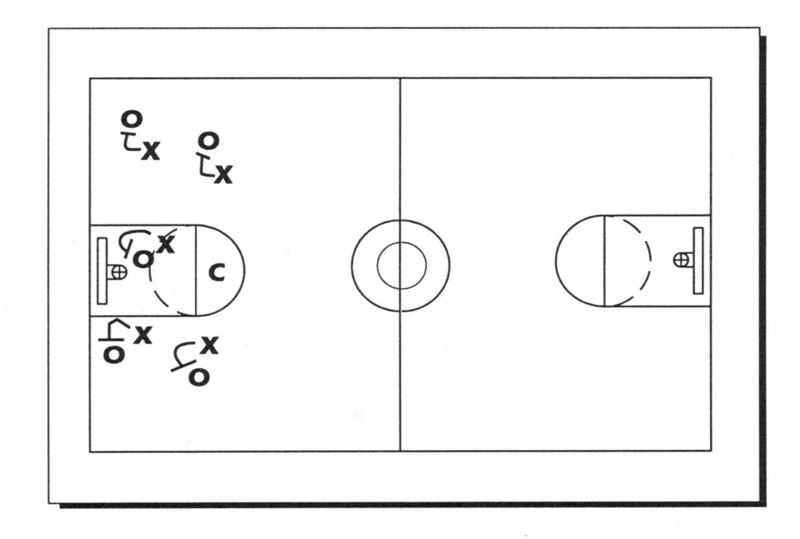

Drill #38: Never Quit

Objective: To teach multiple efforts in securing rebounds.

Description: This drill may use two, three or four pairs of players with each pair being composed of one offensive player and one defensive player. The players are paired with the offensive players facing the basket and the defensive players assuming a good defensive stance. The coach begins the drill by shooting and intentionally missing a shot. The offensive players attempt to rebound and the defensive players box out first and then rebound. If the offense rebounds, the offensive player puts the ball back up immediately from the spot of the rebound. If the defense rebounds, the defender outlets the basketball to the closest wing area. After the first shot is intentionally missed, a second shot is attempted by a second coach. Subsequent shots are taken by the two coaches as the shots are made by the offense or outletted by the defense. The defense continually attempts to hold their box out of the offensive players.

Coaching Points:

- This drill teaches the offense to make multiple attempts to gain a rebound, and it teaches the defense to hold their box-out position longer and more effectively.
- The desire of the players in this drill should be the major point of emphasis.

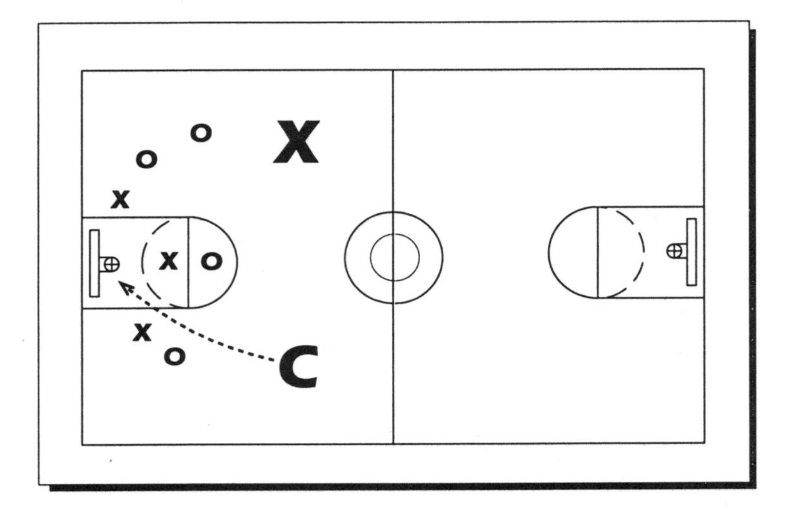

Drill #39: Survive and Thrive

Objective: To teach rebounding technique and aggressiveness.

Description: Divide the team into groups of between four and eight players. Each group is at a basket with three players actively participating in the drill at one time. The three players position themselves in an arc around the basket and assume a proper rebounding stance. A coach or player begins the drill by shooting from the area of the free throw line (subsequent shots should be taken from different angles) and intentionally missing the shot to create a rebound situation. All three players attempt to rebound the missed shot without fouling the other players. The player who rebounds the ball becomes the offensive player and the two other players become the defense. All shots must be taken within the free throw lane. The player also has the option of outletting the ball to the coach and working to get open for a return pass. Once three baskets are made, the player rotates out of the drill and is replaced by another player in the group. The remaining players retain their scores up to that point. Variations include having players lose points for fouling another player or for not playing defense.

Coaching Points:

- When the ball bounces differently than anticipated or the player is unable to get to the best possible location, desire determines if she gets an offensive rebound.

- This drill should emphasize adjusting with the bounce and being aggressive in a controlled manner. The coach should call only the most severe of fouls to avoid dampening the aggressive spirit.

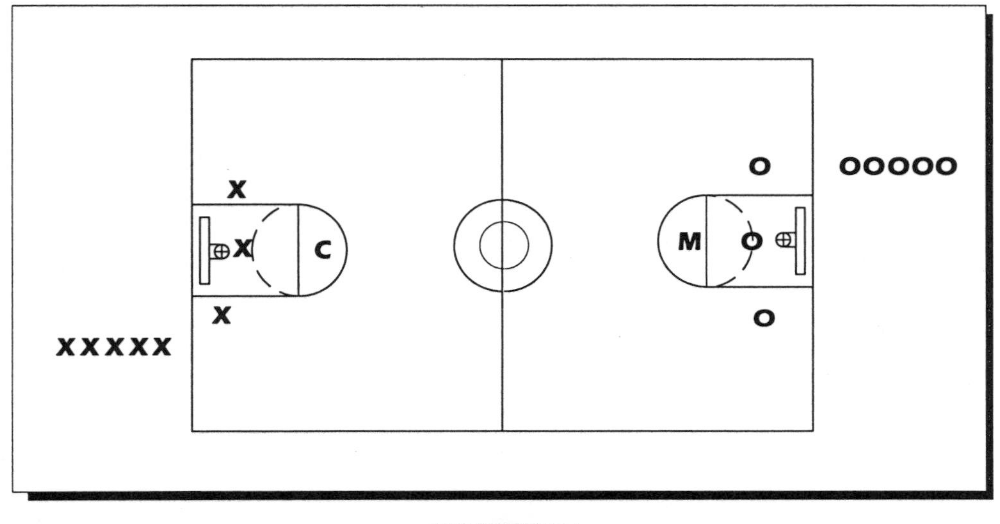

Drill #40: Offensive Imagination

Objective: To practice footwork and offensive rebounding techniques.

Description: This drill involves the entire team participating at one time. Position the players across the half court area radiating outward from the basket in five lines facing the basket. Players should be spaced apart with sufficient distance between players to allow for movement. The coach is in the center of the free throw lane in a position to observe all of the players. On a designated signal from the coach, all of the players execute the appropriate footwork (the swim or spin technique) and move in a designated direction. Variations include adding an imaginary rebound and follow up shot with a head fake.

Coaching Points:

- Proper technique in either of the two moves should first be learned under the controlled situations offered in this drill. The addition of a defensive opponent too soon may cause a player to revert back to her old habits rather than learning the new one presented in this drill.

- The proper techniques of rebounding should be mastered before full speed action is introduced.

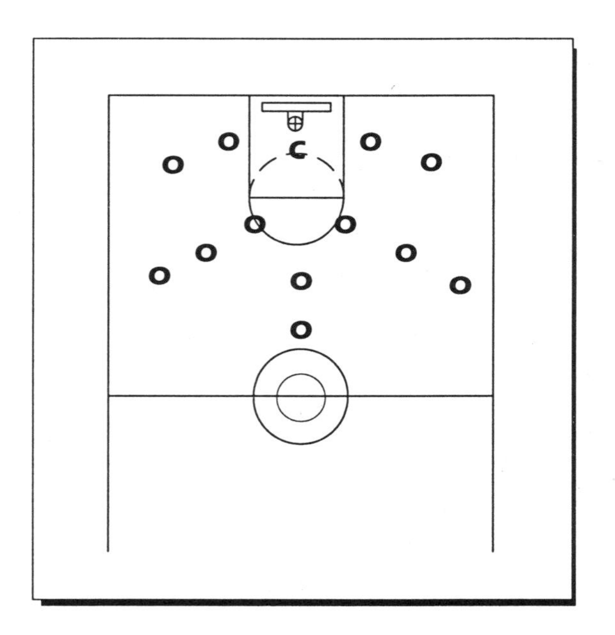

Drill #41: Go-For-It

Objective: To teach boxing out; to develop aggressiveness in rebounding; to practice the outlet pass.

Description: Divide the team into two groups and position them in lines that put the first person in each line at the elbow. Two players are selected to be the defensive players with one defending the first person in each line. A rebounding ring is suggested for the basket. A player or coach should be positioned in the outlet area on either side of the floor. A coach should begin the drill by taking a shot from the floor. The two offensive players crash the boards and the two defensive players practice boxing out. Upon rebounding the ball, the defensive player outlets the ball to the wing. The offensive players then take their places at the end of their lines, while the defensive players get ready for the next pair of offensive players. One pair of defensive players goes against the entire line of offensive players before a change is made.

Coaching Points:

- The angle and location of the shot should be varied to give different "looks" for the players rebounding the basketball.
- Permitting more than the usual amount of pushing and shoving will help the players adjust to game-like situations and to become tougher and more aggressive in rebounding situations.

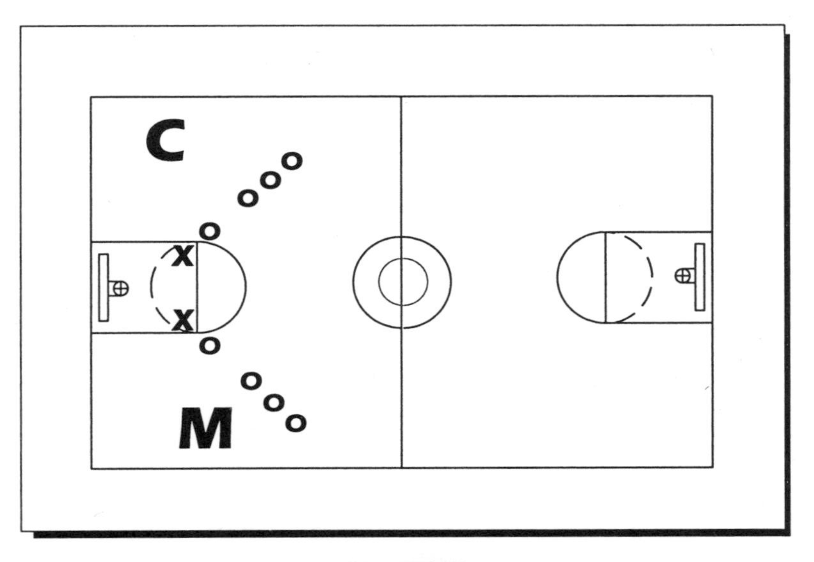

Drill #42: Rebound and Outlet

Objective: To teach strong outlet passing to various locations of the court; to practice rebounding.

Description: Position one rebounder and one coach on each side of the basket in the low post area. Two defensive players are positioned near the division line of the court. The remaining players are equally divided between the low wing areas on both sides of the court. These players break out and serve as the receivers of the outlet pass. The coach designates the type of outlet pass (overhead, bounce, baseball, etc.) to be thrown and whether a dribble is permitted. The ball is then bounced off the backboard, rebounded and the outlet pass thrown to the cutting player on the wing. Adjustments are made by the defensive players to pose different situations to the outlet passer. Each rebounder should throw approximately ten passes before rotating out.

Coaching Points:

- This drill should stress awareness of the defense and good judgement about whether a pass can be completed to a given location and within a specific time frame.
- The coach may also add to the drill by defending the rebounder immediately after the rebound is made.
- Emphasis should be on the completion of a safe, effective outlet pass.

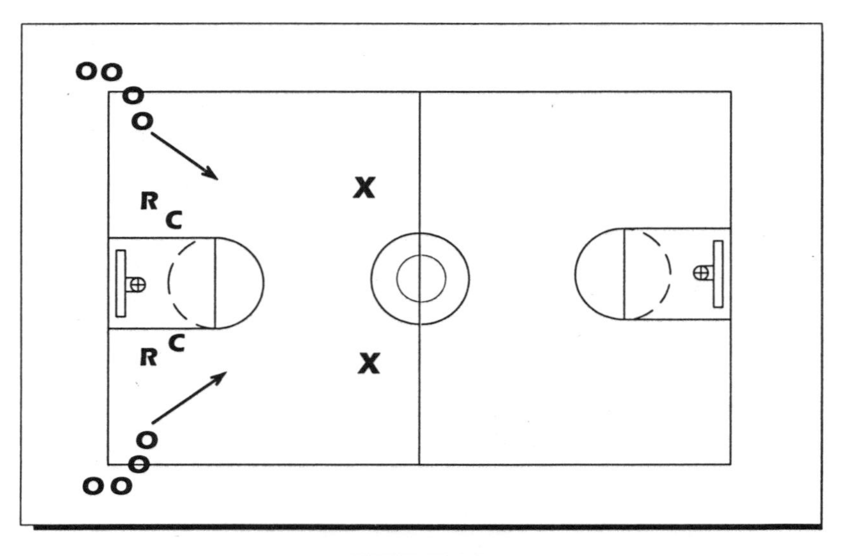

Drill #43: Rotate and Rebound

Objective: To practice rebounding under game-like conditions.

Description: The drill involves three offensive and three defensive players. One player is positioned at the top of the key and one player on each of the two wings. The offensive players are on the outside facing the basket, while the defensive players assume a loose defensive stance. A rebounding ring is suggested. As the coach shoots the ball and calls out either "left" or "right," the defensive players rotate according to the call and box out the player to their immediate left or right. The offensive players move toward the basket in an attempt to rebound the missed shot.

Coaching Points:

- Emphasis should be on teaching the defensive players to box out the player nearest to them when a shot is taken.
- Defensive players should practice calling out "shot" to alert everyone to the fact that a shot has been taken and the need for boxing out is immediate.

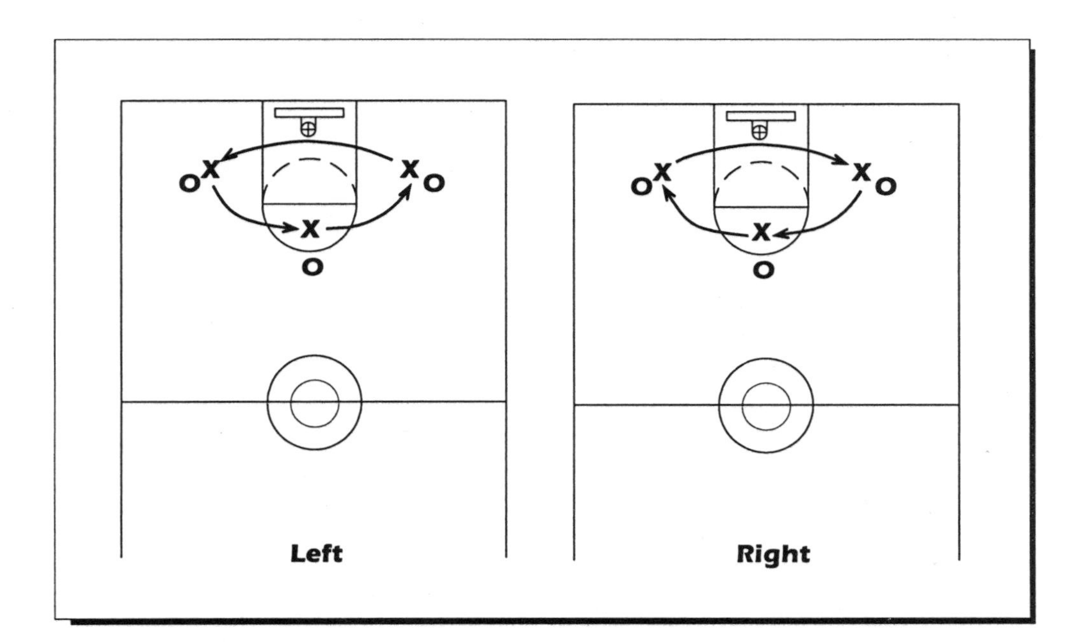

Drill #44: Sandwich Rebounding

Objective: To develop concentration while rebounding; to practice shooting while being fouled; to practice getting the "long" rebound.

Description: Three players take their positions in front of the basket. The middle player is in the "sandwich" and has a basketball. She begins the drill by tossing the ball off the backboard in a manner so the ball comes right back. The player makes the rebound and proceeds to go right back up for the lay up. The players on each side of the middle player foul the shooter but do not attempt to block the shot. Each player should take at least five rebounds before rotating out of the sandwich.

Coaching Point:

- The coach should allow the side players to foul at a level that does not absolutely prohibit the shot, but gives the shooting player enough contact to become accustomed to physical contact during game play (minor slaps on the arms, for example). This practice can help a shooting player overcome the minor contact that may not be called during game play.

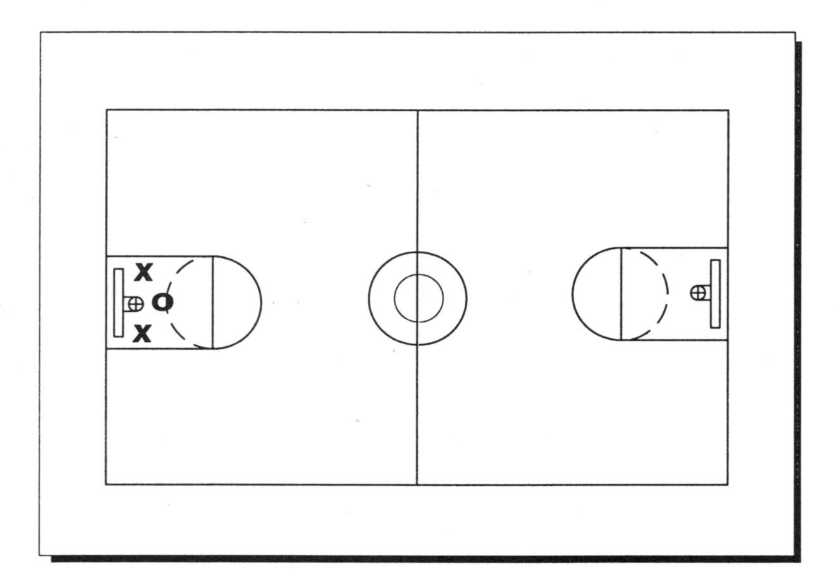

OUT-OF-BOUNDS PLAY DRILLS

Drill #45: Inbound Modified Box Set

Objective: To inbound the ball from the baseline.

Description: Position the players in a modified box with players on the low blocks and the elbows of the free throw lane. The low block player on the ball side sets slightly higher than her counterpart on the opposite side of the lane. This drill involves a two-option play. The first option has the weakside low block person cutting hard toward the basket. The strongside high player and the strongside block player set staggered screens for the weakside high player. She cuts around the two screens to the wing area to receive the pass from the baseline. She is free to shoot from that position. If she does not have a shot from that area the second option includes the weakside block person and the original strongside high player setting a second set of staggered screens in the free throw lane for the inbound passer to circle around for a return pass from the wing area.

Coaching Points:

- For this play to be effective, the cuts should be crisp and the screens should be set in the proper manner. The staggered nature of the screens decreases the effectiveness of switching by the defense.
- The shooter should practice receiving the ball, squaring to the basket, and shooting quickly.

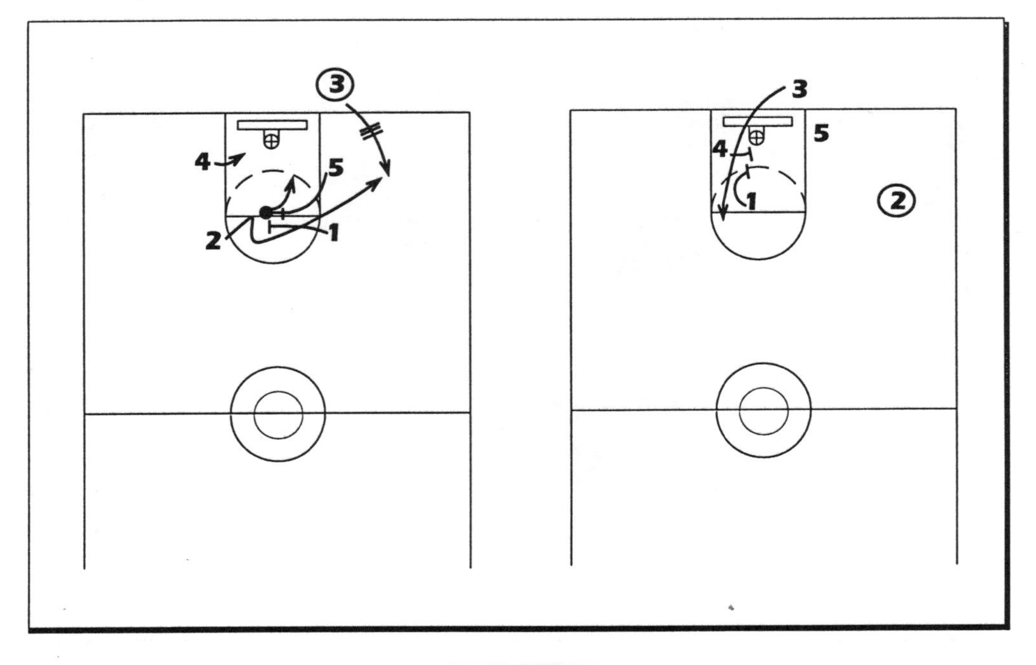

Drill #46: Inbound Random Set

Objective: To inbound the ball from the baseline.

Description: This play uses the backscreen lob as an option to score. One player is located on both the strongside and weakside wings of the half court. The other two players are in a stacked position at the top of the key slightly to the strong side of the floor. The strongside wing breaks toward the lane and then out to the lower wing area. The initial pass is into this wing player and the subsequent pass to the top player from the stack is made without looking for a shot. The top player has broken from her starting position toward the strongside wing player to facilitate the pass. The top player from the stack dribbles toward the weak side of the floor to set up the two scoring options. The first option is developed when the weakside wing sets a backscreen for the lower player in the stack. This player cuts toward the basket down the side of the lane for a possible lob pass from the top of the key. The weakside screener and the strong side low wing set staggered screens for the inbound passer coming from the low block area on the original strong side. This creates a shot opportunity from the elbow of the free throw lane.

Coaching Point:

- The first and second passes should be made quickly and the player from the top of the stack should dribble into position as soon as possible. The backscreen by the weakside wing and her stagger screen on the lower block should also occur quickly.

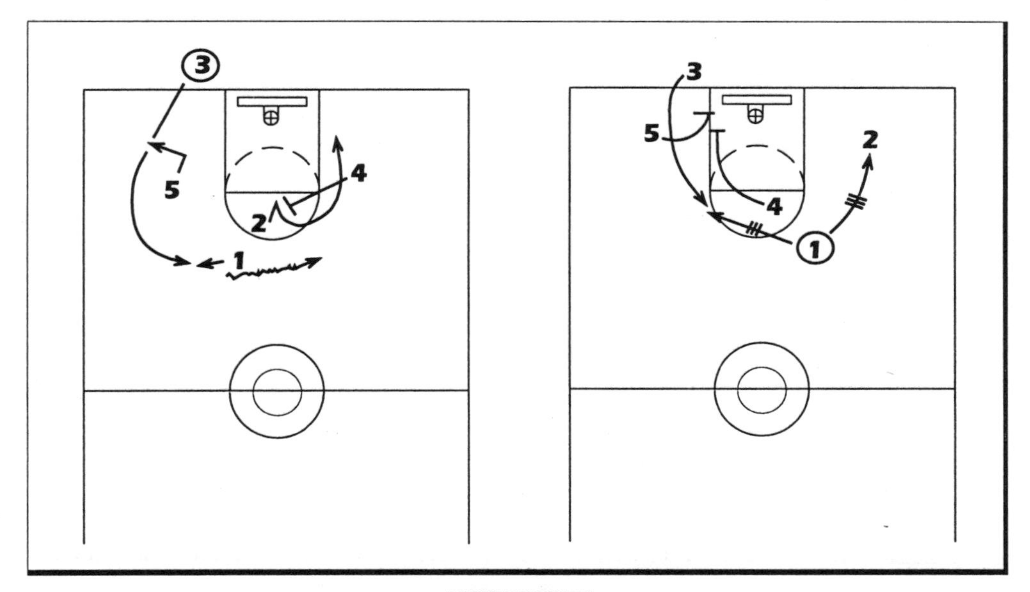

Drill #47: Inbound Stack Set

Objective: To inbound the ball from the baseline.

Description: Position three players along, but outside, the side line of the free throw lane on the same side from which the ball will be inbounded. The remaining player, normally a team's best shooter, is positioned in the weakside corner of the half court. This drill involves a two-option play. At the beginning of the play, the inbound passer may look to the weakside corner for the inbound pass and subsequent shot. The players in the stack all make their moves simultaneously. The lowest player in the stack breaks toward the strongside corner; the middle player in the stack breaks to the middle of the lane near the basket; and the top player in the stack breaks directly toward the inbound passer stopping in the area of the low block on the free throw lane. The second option for the inbound passer involves passing the ball to the strongside corner and cutting off a screen by the player in the center of the free throw lane out to the elbow. The pass from the corner may be made to the top player who has cut to the lower block area or to the inbound passer who has cut off the screen. This player may also shoot off the initial pass.

Coaching Points:

- Faking to one area and having the patience to wait for the second option should be emphasized.
- The strongside corner passer must look quickly for the pass into the low block player to be successful, while the inbound passer must make good use of the screen for the second option to open.

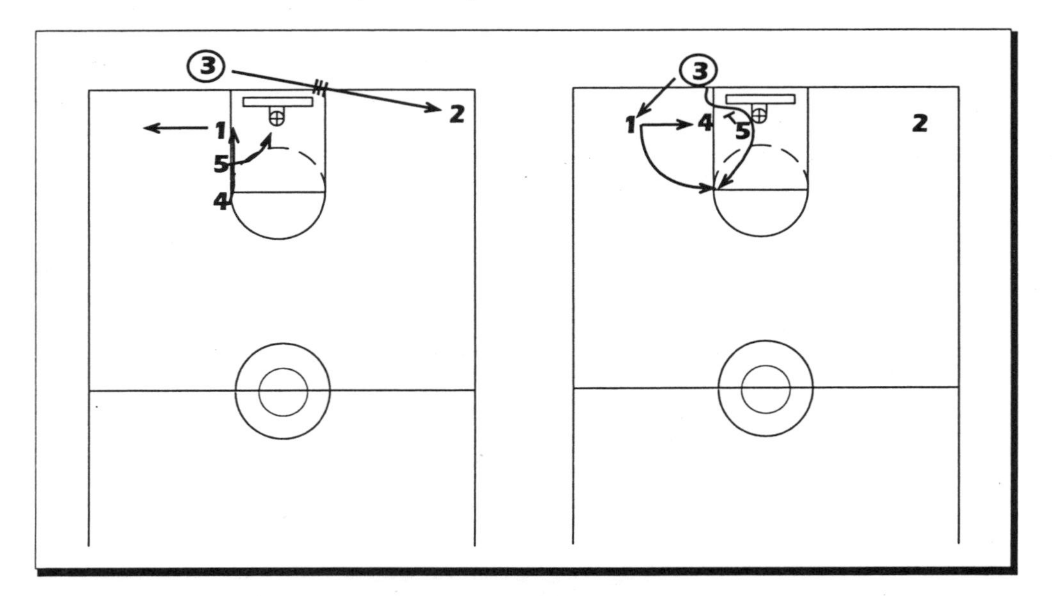

Drill #48: Inbound Box Set

Objective: To inbound the ball from the baseline.

Description: Position the players in a box with players on the low blocks of the free throw lane and at the elbow. As the strongside low block player cuts across the free throw lane to the side opposite the ball, the high strongside player cuts into and then out of the free throw lane and receives a pass in the strongside wing area. Both the low block players turn and face the free throw lane. With the ball on the strongside wing, the weakside high player cuts to the top of the key to receive a reverse pass. After passing the ball to the wing area, the inbound passer circles the two low block players and makes herself available in the free throw lane for a pass from the top of the key. The lower of the two low block players follows the cut of the inbound passer into the free throw lane to provide a second option from the top of the key.

Coaching Points:

- In the second and third passes, faking the ball before passing and accuracy when making the pass should be emphasized.
- Both the cuts by the inbound passer and the low block player should be sharp and come directly off the back of the weakside low block player.
- The second cutter should have some spacing between her and the first cutter, but should enter the lane as soon as the defense has committed to the first cutter.

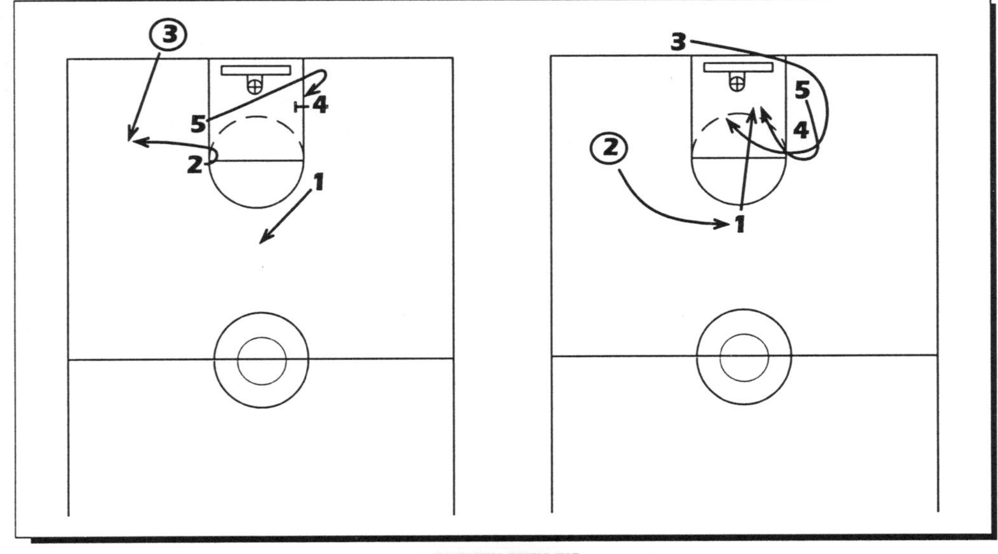

Drill #49: Inbound Side Out

Objective: To inbound the ball from the side line.

Description: Inbounding the ball from the side line presents different problems for the offense than inbounding from the base line. Position two players in the traditional guard spots on either side of the top of the key. The remaining two players are stacked in the low block area of the strong side of the half court. The strongside guard goes across and screens for the weakside guard who cuts toward the ball and receives the inbound pass. She continues to dribble toward the strongside wing, but reverses the ball via the pass to the original screener. The ball is dribbled to the weakside wing to set up the two options of this play. The first option is the low player from the strongside stack cuts to the free throw line and the second option comes from the inbound passer cutting around the low side of the stack and underneath the basket.

Coaching Point:

- Reversing the ball to the screener forces the defense to switch direction and provides the offense a momentary advantage. For this advantage to be maintained, the two cutters have to beat the reaction of the defense to the reversal of the ball.

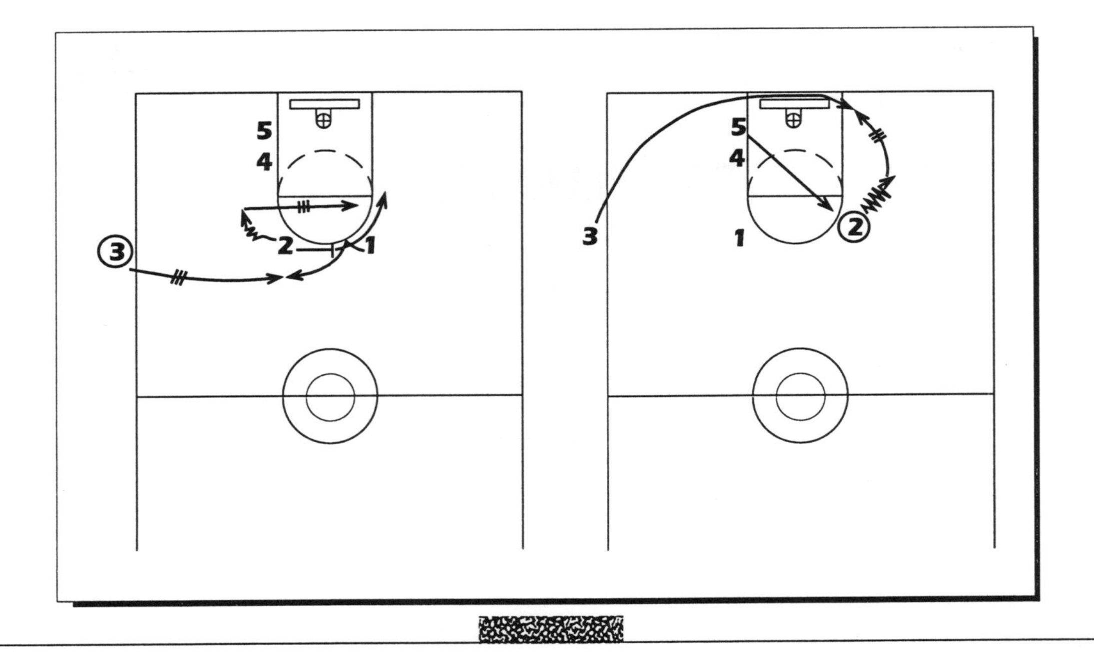

TRANSITION DRILLS

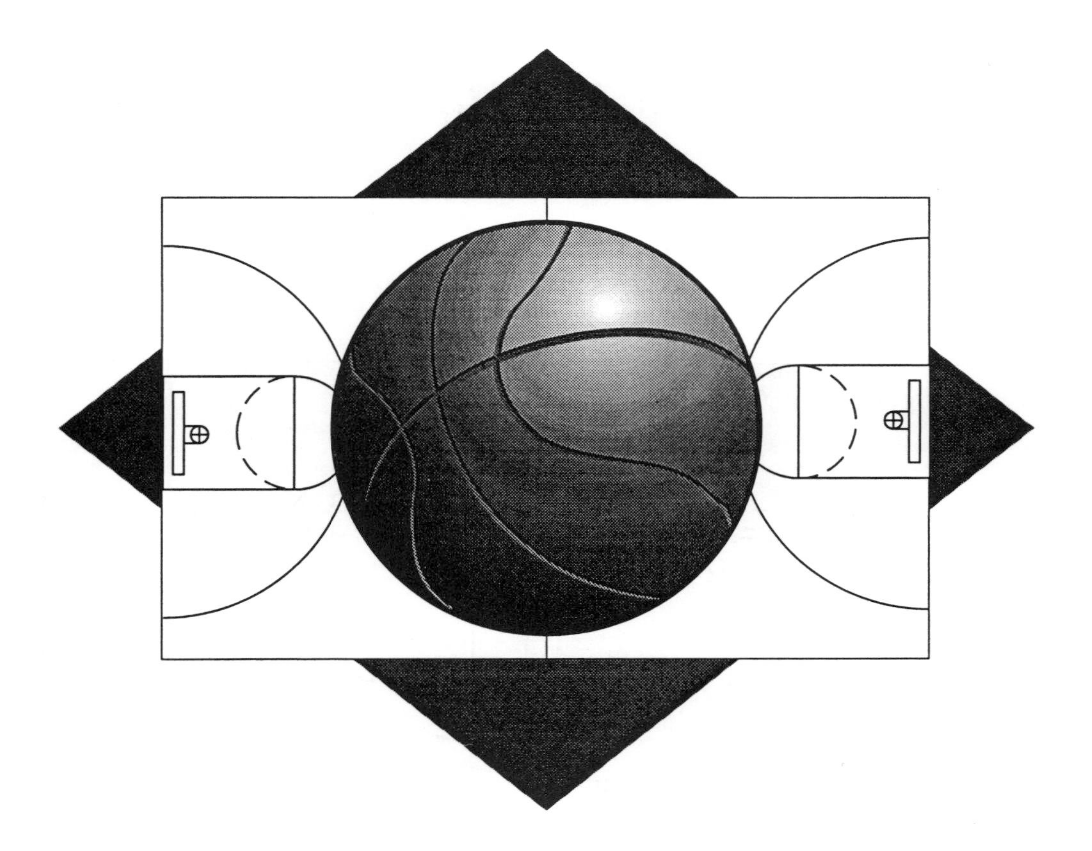

Drill #50: Transition Defense

Objective: To teach the transition from offense to defense.

Description: Position five players in a traditional set of two guards, two forwards and one post player. Position three players out of bounds on one side of the court. One player should be even with the top of the key, one at the division line, and the third even with the opposite midpost area. The coach begins the drill with the ball in the corner on the same side as the three players positioned out of bounds. The drill begins with the coach passing the ball to the first of the three players in line. The defense retreats to the opposite end of the court with the ballside forward challenging the player with the ball. The ballside guard sprints down the floor to the corner of the court on the side down which the ball is being passed. The ball is passed to the center player and the forward follows the pass and maintains pressure on the ball. The ballside post player sprints down the floor to the low post area of the court on the side down which the ball is being passed. The ball is passed to the third player in line and the ballside guard prevents any penetration from her corner position. The offside guard sprints down the court to the top of the opposite key and prevents the ball from being reversed to the weakside of the court. The weakside forward sprints to the low post area opposite the ballside post player to prevent a weakside lob pass or a pass across the baseline.

Coaching Points:

- In effective transition defense, each player should have an assigned position to cover and responsibilities associated with those areas.
- Each task and responsibility should be explained in detail and understood before players move out of this drill.

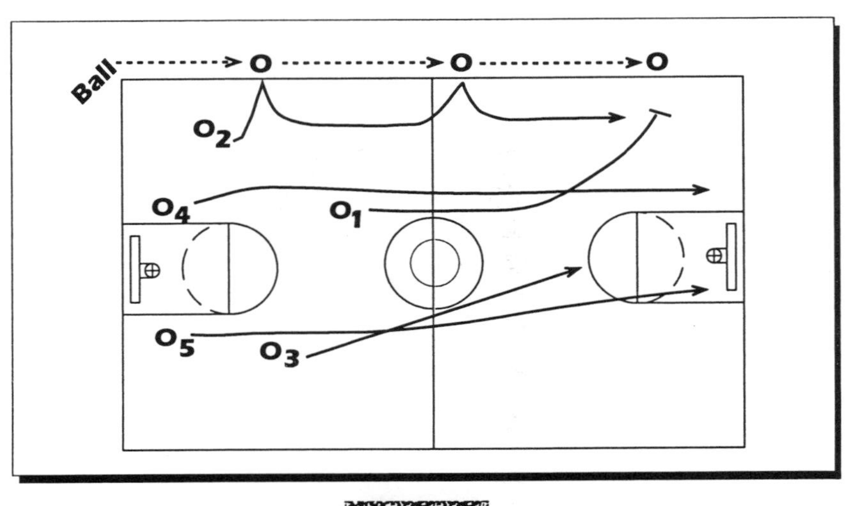

Drill #51: Free Throw Transition

Objective: To practice transitioning after a free throw.

Description: This drill may be run off either a made or a missed free throw attempted by the coach. The five offensive and five defensive players line up on the free throw lane as if an actual free throw were to be taken (one offensive player lines up as the shooter). The remaining players are positioned outside the top of the key. If the shot is missed, the four defensive players screen out the three offensive players on the free throw lane and the shooter. One of the two inside players rebounds the ball and outlets it to the closest wing. This player should break from her spot on the lane to receive the pass. The ball is advanced to the middle of the floor by passing to the person at the top of the key or by dribbling the ball to the center of the floor. In either situation, the remaining two outside players fill the lanes for the transition to the fast break. If the shot is made, one of the lower players on the free throw lane takes the ball out of bounds and inbounds the ball to one of the three outside players. The ball is then centered on the court via either a pass or a dribble. The other two outside players fill the lane for the fast break.

Coaching Points:

- Assigned movements under given conditions will help minimize confusion and ease the transition into the fast break.
- Permitting the offensive team to try to disrupt the transition by denying passing lanes and/or preventing the outlet pass adds reality to the drill.

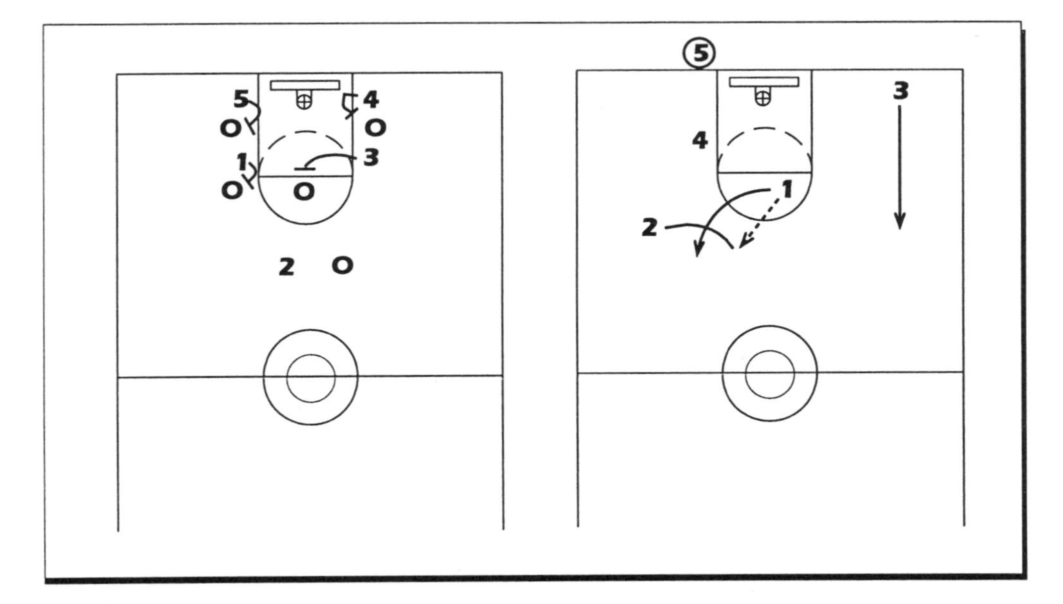

Drill #52: Tandem Defensive Transition

Objective: To teach fast-break defense and conversion from defense to offense.

Description: Position two defensive players at one end of the full court with one on the free throw line and the other in the center of the free throw lane facing the opposite end of the court. Divide the team into three groups and space them on the base line opposite the defenders. Each person in the middle line should have a basketball. The middle player passes to the player in the right line and goes behind her to fill the right lane of the fast break. The receiver passes to the player in the left wing who has broken to middle of the free throw circle and then cuts behind her to fill the left lane of the fast break. These three players continue down the court in a classic 3-on-2 fast break situation. Two possible scenarios can arise. If one of the three offensive players completes the fast break by making a shot, the two defenders take the ball out of the basket and break 2-on-1 against the shooter to the other end of the court. The remaining two offensive players rotate to become the next two defenders. If a shot is missed and rebounded by the defense, the two defenders fast break to the other end of the court against the shooter. The remaining offensive players rotate to become the next two defenders. In either case, the next three people in line begin the next set as soon as the 2-on-1 has been completed at their end of the court.

Coaching Points:

- Being prepared to transition from offense to defense and vice versa after a shot should be stressed during this drill.
- Delays in transition can have substantial effects on an up-tempo game plan.

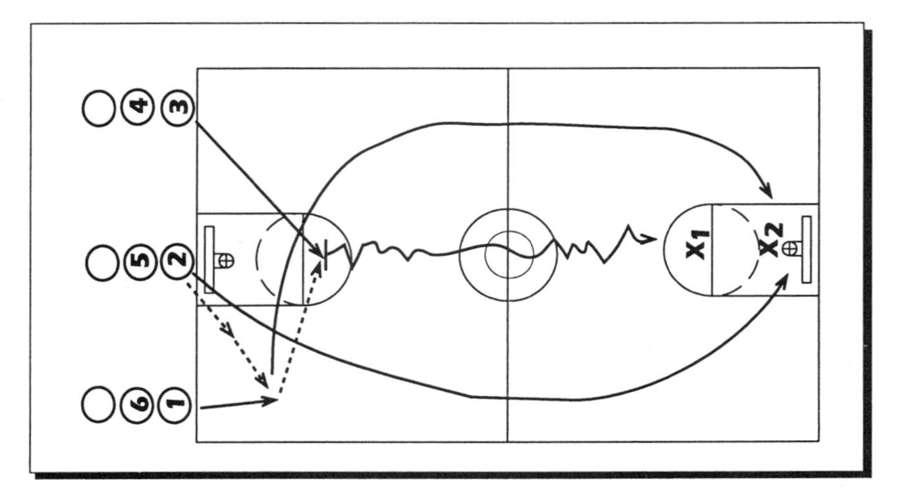

Drill #53: Retreat and Defeat

Objective: To teach a two-defender tandem how to retreat effectively.

Description: Divide the team into three lines and position them across one base line facing the full court. The first person in each line is then repositioned on the end of the court nearest the three lines and spaced across the free throw line extended facing the baseline. These three players are on defense. The coach, standing on the free throw line, tosses the basketball to the first person in one of the three lines. This action begins the drill. That player and the first person in the other two lines begin a fast break by moving the ball to the middle and filling the lanes. The defensive player directly in front of the player who received the pass from the coach must move forward to the base line and touch the line before retreating on defense. The other two defenders retreat on defense as soon as the first pass is made. A 3-on-2 situation ensues until the third defender can recover. The coach goes to the opposite end and repeats the drill using the same three players on offense and the same three players on defense.

Coaching Points:

- The offensive players should learn to travel the floor and execute the shot while they still have the advantage, while the defense must learn how to best defend the 3-on-2 offensive thrust long enough for help to arrive.
- The third defensive player learns that through hustling down the floor her specific efforts can make a difference.

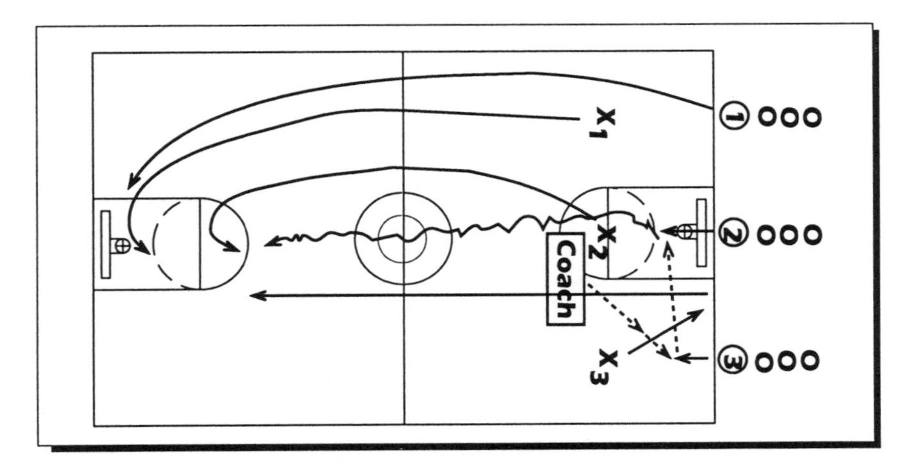

Drill #54: Three-On-Three-On-Three

Objective: To teach fast break defense and conversion to a pressing defense.

Description: Position three players at each end of the court—two players in tandem defense in the free throw lane and the third player out to one side near the side line. These two groups of players are designated groups A and B for the purposes of explanation. Three additional players (group C) are spaced across the division line facing one end of the full court. Group C begins the drill by going 3-on-2 against the two defensive players from group B. Two scenarios may arise: First, if the two players from group B stop the fast break, they outlet the ball to the third member of their group and fast break to the other end against two members of group A. Second, if group C scores a basket, they immediately go into a full court press against group B. Group C may double-team or zone press, but may only go up to the division line of the full court. At that point group B continues to offensively attack against group A (full three players). Group A may only advance to play defense up to the 28-foot mark on the floor. The drill continues as a three-on-three drill with the same two possible scenarios possible. Keeping score will add competition to this drill.

Coaching Points:

- The major point to be stressed is the rapid transition from offense to defense and the advantages of beating the other team in that transition.

- The drill also prepares the offensive team by advancing the ball against the defense of six players rather than five.

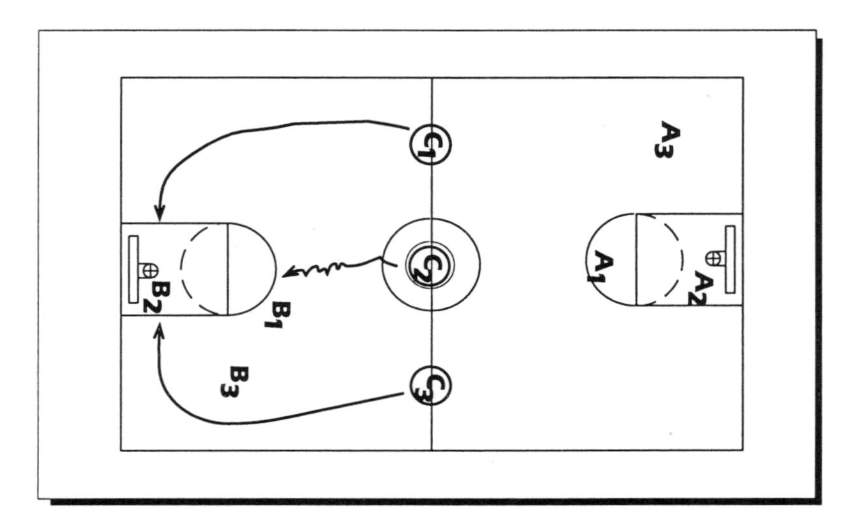

BASIC DEFENSIVE FUNDAMENTALS DRILLS

Drill #55: Sprint and Slide

Objective: To improve conditioning; to practice defensive foot positioning.

Description: The drill involves one player at a time. The player assumes a proper defensive position in one corner facing the inside of the rectangular space. The player moves along the side of the rectangular space to the other corner. Upon reaching the corner, the player sprints diagonally across the space to the opposite corner. The player then reassumes a proper defensive position and slides along the side of the rectangular space to the other corner. Upon reaching the corner, the player sprints diagonally across the space to the opposite corner returning to the initial starting point for the drill.

Coaching Points:

- If this drill is done utilizing the entire half court space, it emphasizes the maintenance of good footwork and a proper defensive position over an extended period of time and space.

- The drill can be used as a conditioning drill by lengthening the time spent doing the drill. The drill should stress the importance of maintaining a proper defensive position even when a player is tired.

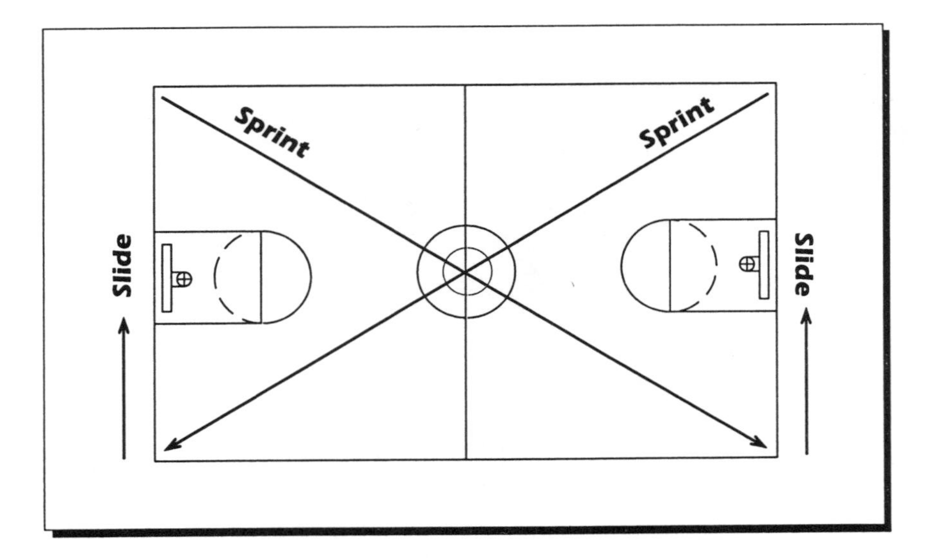

Drill 56: Defensive Sliding Drill

Objective: To teach defensive sliding, cutting off the dribbler and hand position.

Description: Four dribblers and four defensive players begin the drill by positioning themselves on one baseline equally spaced across the entire width of the court. Each pair of players works inside an imaginary lane approximately ten feet wide. The dribbler proceeds the length of the court by zigzagging from side to side within the imaginary lane. The defensive players utilizes a good defensive stance, quick slides of the feet and proper hand position to cut off the offensive player and cause a reversal of direction. Early attempts at this drill should concentrate on foot positioning and speed rather than stealing the basketball. The steal portion of the drill is normally added at a later stage. Upon reaching the opposite end of the court the players reverse positions and repeat the drill in the opposite direction.

Coaching Points:

- The defensive player should concentrate on reaching with the lead foot to cut off the dribbler and using two quick steps to beat the offensive player to a particular spot on the floor.

- The defensive player's movements must be done quickly from a balanced position. A defensive player who does not maintain balance will be beaten by a dribbling offensive player because it is difficult to maintain active, quick movements of the feet without maintaining a good, balanced position.

- The player should keep the hands in a ready position to steal the ball and the first opportunity. Proper hand/arm position also aids the defensive player in reacting quickly to the moves of the offensive player by providing a good, balanced defensive stance.

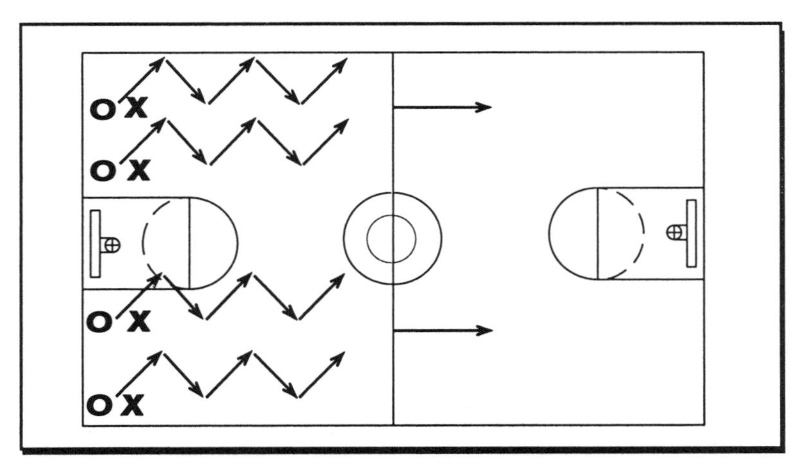

Drill #57: Post Denial

Objective: To teach denial of a pass from a wing and the corner to the post.

Description: Two offensive players are positioned on one side of the court—one even with the free throw line in the wing area; the other in the corner of the court. A third offensive player is positioned outside the lane approximately six feet from the baseline. These three players, representing the offensive team, are defended by two defensive players. One of the defenders attacks the ball when it is in possession of either the wing or the corner offensive player. The other defensive player attempts to prevent the pass from entering the post area by playing good pass-denial defense. If the pass into the post is successful, the outside defensive player collapses to assist the post defender. When the ball is passed from the post to the wing or the corner, the defender goes and attacks the ball.

Coaching Points:

- The post defender should step in front of the post and deny the entry pass. By either foot or arm position she should maintain a presence in the passing lane regardless of the position of the ball. This requires her to beat the post player to spots on the floor and maintain eye contact with the post player and the ball at all times.

- The outside defender can assist her teammate by aggressively attacking the ball in both the wing and the corner position. She can also assist the post defender by double teaming the offensive post player in the event the pass to the post is successful. This denies the offense the higher percentage shot and forces them to pass the ball back to the wing or the corner.

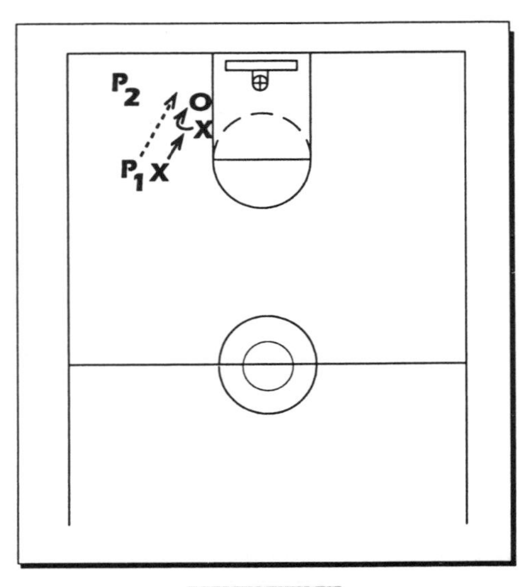

Drill #58: Flash Denial

Objective: To defend the pass into the post position in both the high and low post.

Description: One offensive player assumes a position on the wing, while a second offensive player is placed in the corner of the court on the same side. A post player that will be defended assumes a position on the low side of the free throw lane on the opposite side of the court. The defensive player assumes a good weakside defensive position in the center of the free throw lane. The offensive player being defended flashes across the lane to the opposite elbow to provide a good passing target for the wing. If denied at that location, the ball is passed from the wing to the corner and the offensive post player spins toward the low post in an effort to provide a good passing target for the player in the corner.

Coaching Points:

- The defender must defend the "high side" of the post to prevent the pass from the wing, and then beat the post player to the low post to prevent the pass from the corner.
- To properly defend the pass from the corner, the defender must not only beat the post player to the low post area, but must also be able to switch arms and position from the "high side" to the "low side".
- The drill should stress assuming the defensive position on the low side so that if the pass enters the post, the offensive player if forced to the middle where defensive help should be available.

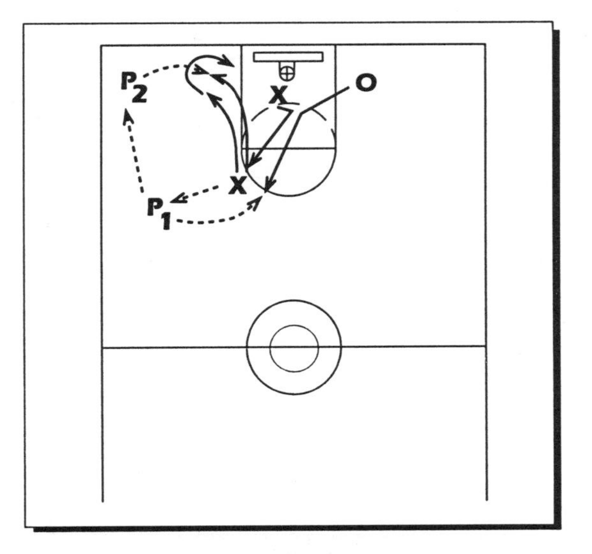

Drill #59: Help Rotation 1

Objective: To provide weakside help defense; to practice regaining the proper defensive position.

Description: Four offensive players are positioned—one player at each of the elbows and one player in each of the low corners of the half court. Two defensive players assume good defensive positions in the midpost area while straddling the outside line of the free throw lane. The primary defensive assignment for the two players is the two offensive players in the corners. The ball moves from either point player to one of the corner players. The offensive player then attempts to drive the baseline. The weakside defensive player comes across the lane to help defend against the drive. If the offensive player is stopped, the ball is reversed to the opposite point player, and an attempt is made to pass the ball to the opposite corner player. The weakside defender who provided defensive help must recover across the lane and deny the pass to the corner player. If the pass is completed, the defenders have switched roles, and the play occurs on the other side.

Coaching Points:

- The weakside defender should maintain contact with her offensive player and the ball at all times. When her teammate is in danger of being beaten, she should come to assist her teammate to prevent the lay-up.

- After completing the help defense and denying the driving lane, the weakside defensive player must recover in time to prevent the reversal of the ball to the opposite corner for a short jumpshot. The original strongside defender then becomes the weakside defender and should be prepared to assist from the weak side in the event of a drive to the basket.

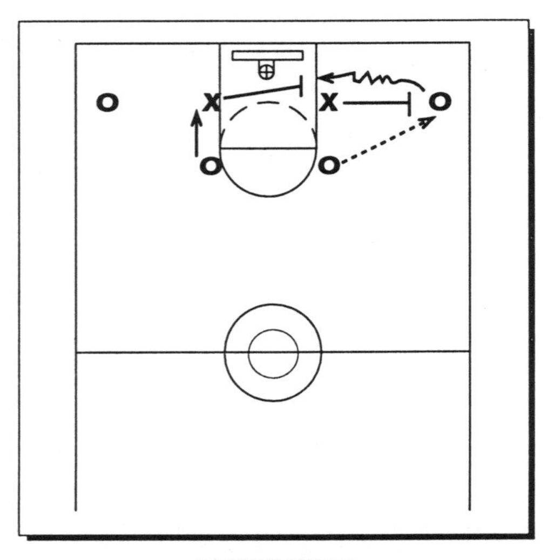

Drill #60: Help Rotation 2

Objective: To teach help defense; to practice the proper defensive rotation to recovery.

Description: This drill requires three offensive players and three defensive players. The offensive players are positioned in each corner and near the elbow. The defensive players are positioned with one player on each side of the lane in the low post and the third at the elbow of the lane opposite the offensive guard. This player begins the drill by passing to the offensive guard. She then becomes a defensive player involved in the help rotation. The offensive guard passes to the ballside corner. This player drives the baseline, beating the defensive player on the strong side of the lane. This defender calls "Help" upon being beaten. The weakside defender person slides across the lane and stops the driving offensive player. The defensive guard is now part of the help rotation and must defend against the weakside forward cutting into the area vacated by the initial helping defender. When the driving forward is stopped and the help rotation is completed, the ball is passed out to the offensive guard. She begins the drill on the opposite side as the original guard resumes her position at the elbow. The same rotation is then done on the opposite side of the floor with the two guards switching roles.

Coaching Points:

- The strongside player should announce her need for help,then rotate her defensive position from the corner to the offensive guard.
- The weakside forward should slide across the lane and stop the dribble penetration to prevent a relatively easy shot.
- The weakside guard should and drop to cover the offensive player/area vacated by the helping forward to prevent a pass across the lane.

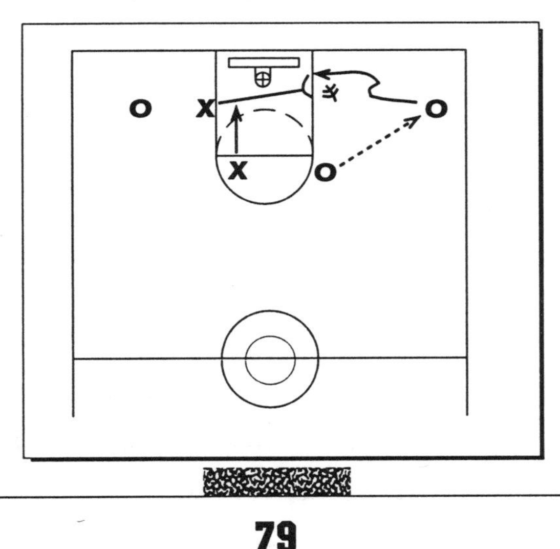

Drill #61: Perimeter Defense

Objective: To practice defending against perimeter passes; to develop the ability to maintain pressure on the ball.

Description: The drill involves three offensive players and three defensive players. One of the offensive players assumes a position at the head of the key, while the other two offensive players are at each of the two wing positions. The three defenders assume a good defensive position on the offensive players. The ball starts in the middle of the floor. Each of the wing players attempts to present a good passing target to the player with the ball. If the ball reaches the wing, the point player then attempts to present a good passing target to the wing player with the ball. The defensive player pressures the ball and denies the passing lane depending on where the ball is located in relation to her offensive player.

Coaching Points:

- When the defender is off the ball, two basic points should be stressed. First, if the ball is one pass away from her offensive player, she should be concerned with denying the passing lane. Second, if the ball is two passes away from her offensive player, the defender should be concerned with providing weakside help in the event of a drive from the strongside of the court.

- When the defender is on the ball, she should attack to maintain pressure on the offensive player and force the player to one side or the other.

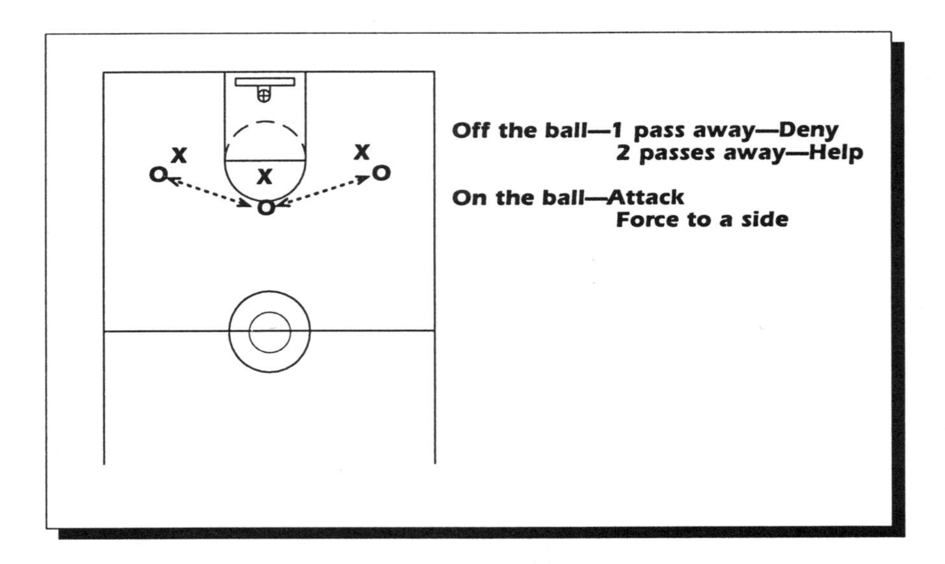

Drill #62: Shell Defense

Objective: To teach perimeter defense.

Description: The drill involves four offensive players and four defensive players. The offensive players assume positions as two guards on either side of the head of the key and two forwards in the low wing areas. The defensive players take up good man-to-man defensive positions. Either guard may start with the ball. The defensive player guarding the ball applies pressure and attempts to disrupt the sight lines for potential passing lanes. The players who are one pass away from the ball guard their respective offensive players in such a way as to maintain one hand in the passing lane at all times. Each offensive player moves to present the best possible passing target for her teammate. As the ball changes location around the court, the defensive players adjust their positions according to their specific responsibilities and whether they are one or two passes away from the ball.

Coaching Points:

- The player guarding the ball should maintain pressure to decrease the offensive player's ability to see the passing lanes and execute successful passes.
- Defensive players who are one pass away from the ball should work to deny the easy pass. The defender who is more than one pass away from the ball should be prepared to provide help defense in the event of a dribble penetration.
- This drill should stress that proper positioning of the defensive player depends on her ability to see both the ball and her offensive player at all times.

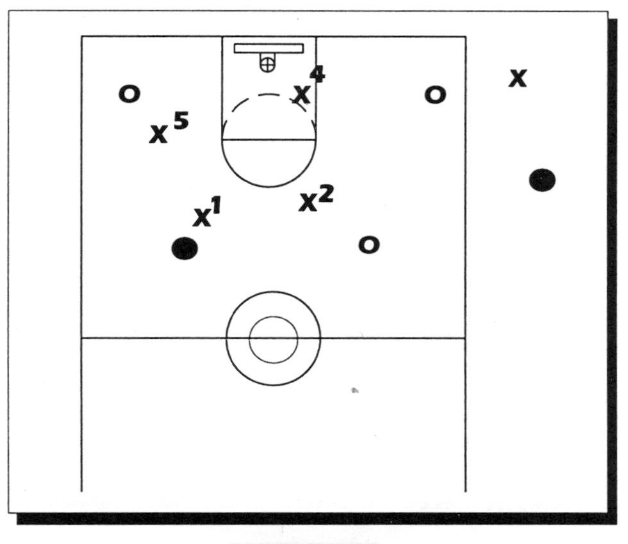

Drill #63: Post Defense

Objective: To prevent the pass into the post player.

Description: The drill involves five players—four offensive players and one defender. Three offensive players are positioned as follows: one is at the head of the key and one on each of the two wing positions. The fourth offensive player starts in the low post position on either side of the free throw lane. The single defender assumes a good defensive position based upon where the ball starts in the drill. The ball is free to move from the point player to either wing in an attempt to pass the ball into the post. The offensive post player is free to move to any position within the free throw lane. The defensive player must remain in a good defensive position and attempt to deny the pass into the post.

Coaching Points:

- The defensive player should rotate around the offensive post player and continually beat the post player to the appropriate spot on the floor. This requires her to have good foot speed and the ability to switch position from one side of the offensive player to the other based on where the pass will come from.

- The switching of the defensive arm in the passing lane should also be stressed. The use of the correct arm will help to effectively deny the pass, while minimizing the possibility of a foul being called on the defender.

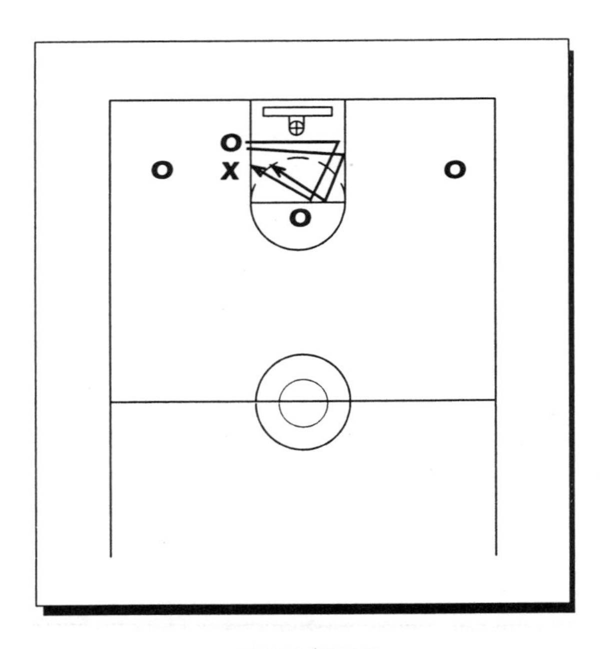

Drill #64: Defending the High Post Screen

Objective: To develop the ability to defend against a high post screen.

Description: The drill involves four players—two on offense and two on defense. The two offensive players are positioned at the head of the key and the high post position at the intersection of the free throw line and the outside line of the free throw lane. The two defensive players assume a good man-to-man defensive position on the two offensive players. The high post player sets a screen for the offensive guard. The guard then attempts to run her defensive player into the screen so that she can clear a path to drive to the basket. The defender covering the high post player intercepts the path of the driving guard and maintains this position long enough to allow her defensive teammate to recover from the screen and resume a good defensive position on the guard with the ball.

Coaching Points:

- The player defending the high post offensive player has three defensive functions to perform if the play is to be stopped. She should move into the path of the dribbling guard to prevent penetration into the free throw lane, hold this defensive position long enough to allow her defensive teammate to recover, and maintain defensive contact with the high post offensive player to prevent the execution of the screen and roll. If any one of these three functions is not completed correctly, the defense breaks down.

- The defensive player covering the guard can either beat the dribbling guard to the spot of the screen (thereby defeating the effectiveness of the screen) or, if she doesn't defeat the screen, she must recover as quickly as possible to prevent the dribble penetration.

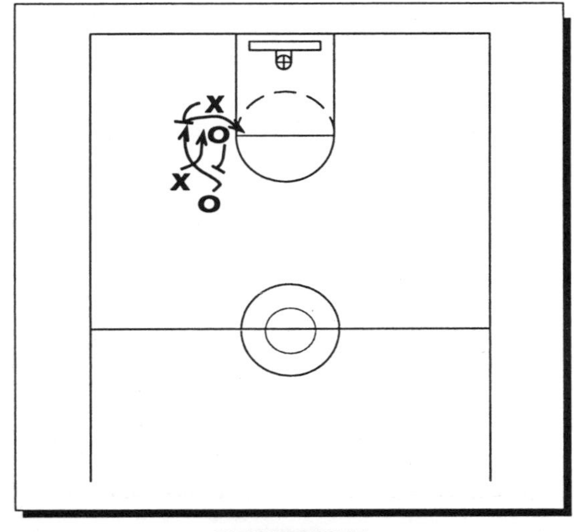

Drill #65: Corner Denial

Objective: To teach denial of the pass from the wing to the post.

Description: The drill involves three players—two on offense and one on defense. One offensive player is given a basketball and assumes a position on either side of the head of the key. A second offensive player is positioned in the wing position. The defensive player assumes a good defensive position between the ball and the wing player. The offensive wing player may move anywhere in the area bounded by her side of the free throw lane, the free throw line extended and the sideline/baseline of the court in an effort to create a favorable passing lane for the passer. The defensive player moves to deny the pass to the wing player. The drill should be conducted on a continuous basis for a minimum of thirty seconds before a new defender rotates into the drill.

Coaching Points:

- The emphasis should be on the defensive player maintaining a proper denial position throughout the drill. The need to move two steps for each step the offensive player makes should also be stressed.

- The defensive player should also concentrate on keeping her hands in the passing lane at all times. This can compensate for any momentary lapses in foot position.

- In order to maintain the denial position, the defensive player should maintain the space between her and the offensive player.

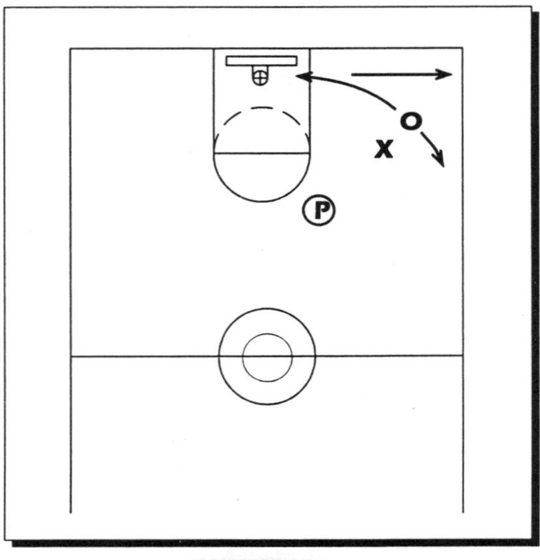

Drill #66: Guard-to-Guard Help and Recover

Objective: To develop the ability to defend against the dribble penetration between the two offensive guards.

Description: The drill involves four individuals—two guards on offense and two players on defense. The two offensive guards are positioned on opposite sides of the top of the key. The two defensive players assume a good defensive position in a man-to-man defensive scheme. The offensive guard opposite the basketball moves across the court and establishes a screening position for her teammate. The guard with the ball moves laterally across the court using the dribble. The primary goal of the defensive players is to stop the dribble in a manner similar to that employed in Drill # 64. After the help and recover situation has been completed, the play is repeated on the opposite side.

Coaching Points:

- The defensive player covering the player setting the screen should jump out and stop the dribble penetration, hold the defensive position long enough for her teammate to recover, and maintain contact with her offensive screener to prevent the screen and roll.

- The defensive player being screened must either beat the dribbler to the screen (thereby, nullifying the effectiveness of the screen) or recover quickly enough to resume a good defensive position.

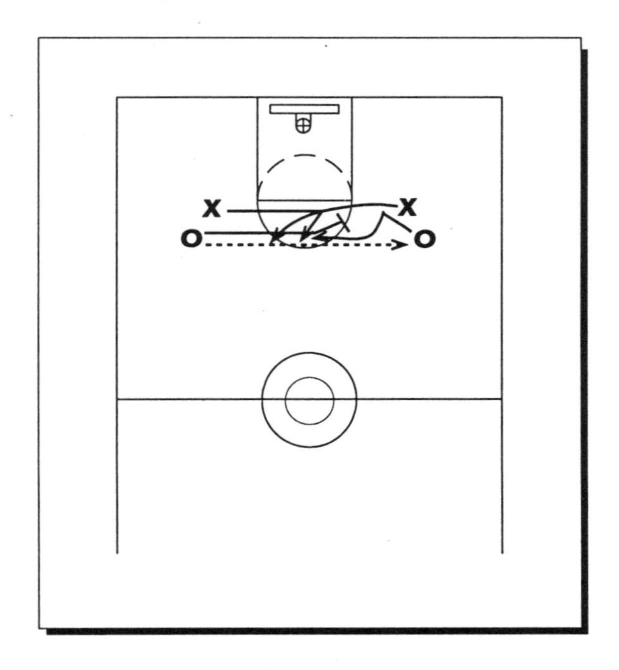

Drill #67: Guard-to-Forward Help and Recover

Objective: To develop the ability to defend against the dribble penetration between an offensive guard and a forward.

Description: The drill involves four players—two on offense and two on defense. One offensive player (a guard) is positioned on the side of the free throw lane extended near the top of the free throw circle. The other offensive player (a forward) is positioned on the same side of the court in the "low wing position." Two defensive players assume good defensive position in a man-to-man defensive scheme. The basketball starts in the hands of the forward. The guard starts the drill by attempting to set a screen on the player guarding the forward. The forward moves away from the baseline using the dribble and the screen of her teammate to accomplish dribble penetration toward the basket. The goal of the defensive players is stop the dribble in a manner similar to that used in Drill #64. After the help and recover situation is completed, the players return to their original spots and the play is repeated.

Coaching Points:

- The defensive player covering the guard who is attempting to set a screen should jump out and stop the dribble penetration by the forward, hold the defensive position long enough for her teammate to recover and maintain contact with her offensive screener to prevent the screen and roll.

- The defensive player being screened must either beat the dribbler to the screen (thereby nullifying the effectiveness of the screen) or recover quickly enough to resume a good defensive position.

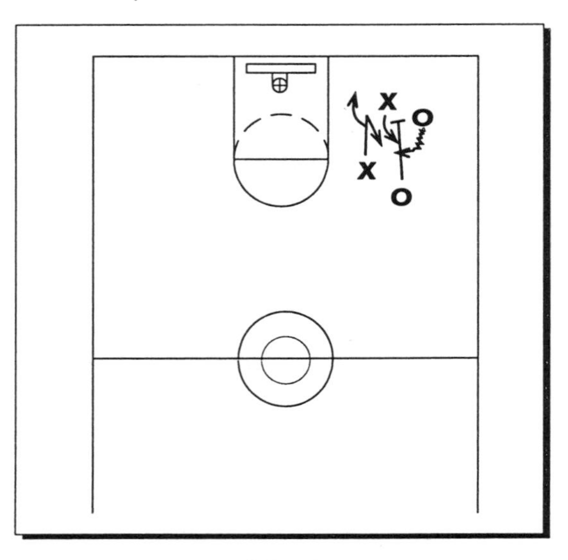

Drill #68: Defensive Slide

Objective: To teach coordinated defense between two defensive guards.

Description: This drill involves two offensive guards and two defensive guards. The two offensive guards are positioned above the head of the key. Either of the offensive guards may start with the basketball. The defensive players assume a good guarding position on their respective players—one player straight up on the ball and the other slightly off in a "help" position. Upon a pass from one offensive player to the other, the two defensive players slide from their initial positions to assume good defensive positions on their respective opponents—one straight up on the ball and the other in the help position. After the slide on the pass between guards has been accomplished, a dribble can be added to the drill.

Coaching Points:

- The defensive player who was straight up on the basketball should quickly slide from her defensive position to a help and recover position. The opposite guard should move quickly from a help position to apply pressure on the ball.
- The coordination and the help/recover parts of this drill should be stressed to facilitate a higher level of team defense at the guard position.

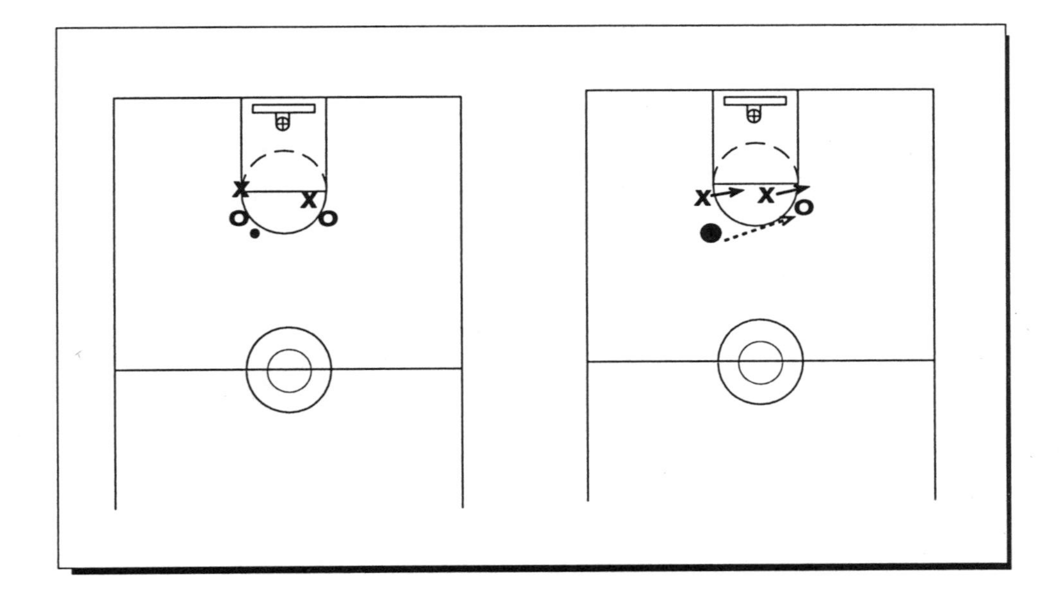

Drill #69: Baseline Full

Objective: To teach defending the pass to the corner position.

Description: The drill involves four players—three on offense and one on defense. Position two of the offensive players in the wing positions. Each of these players should have a basketball. The third offensive player may start in either corner. The defender assumes a good defensive position between the passer and the player she is guarding. The drill begins with the offensive player in the corner being permitted to move the entire width of the court in order to create a favorable passing lane between her and either of the two passers. Anytime the pass is completed, the offensive player squares herself to the basket, passes the basketball back to the passer from whom she received the pass and continues her cuts. Each offensive player and defensive player should spend thirty seconds cutting and denying before they rotate positions in the drill.

Coaching Points:

- Emphasis should be placed on the importance of taking two steps on defense to every one step on offense, using both hands to deny good passing lanes, and maintaining eye contact with the ball and the player being guarded.
- The introduction of the second passer emphasizes the need for good execution by the defense.

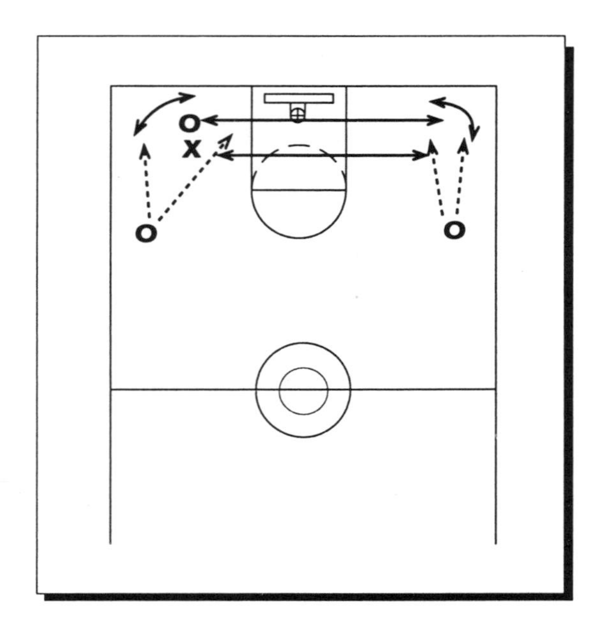

Drill #70: Combo Defense (4-on-4)

Objective: To teach pass denial under a variety of conditions.

Description: The drill involves four offensive players and four defensive players. Position the four offensive players in a shell around the half court. The four defensive players assume a good, tight defensive position on their respective offensive player. The coach begins the drill at the high post position on the free throw line. The offensive players move anywhere they want in an attempt to create a favorable passing lane from the center. Variations on this drill can include any or all of the following: (1) limit the number of passes the offense may take; (2) allow or deny cuts by the offensive team; (3) require that each play must start with a screen and roll by the offense; and (4) designate one offensive player as the shooter. Each of these variations creates different situations for the defense. On the signal to "change" from the coach, the offense and defense switch assignments.

Coaching Points:

- The primary principles of man-to-man defense should be emphasized, including pressure on the ball at all times, deny-defense one pass from the ball, and help-defense two passes from the ball.

- Variety can be incorporated into the drill by either adding a fifth offensive player (thereby forcing the defense to contend with a 5-on-4 situation) or positioning two coaches in the two corners of the court and having them assist the offense by serving as primary passers only.

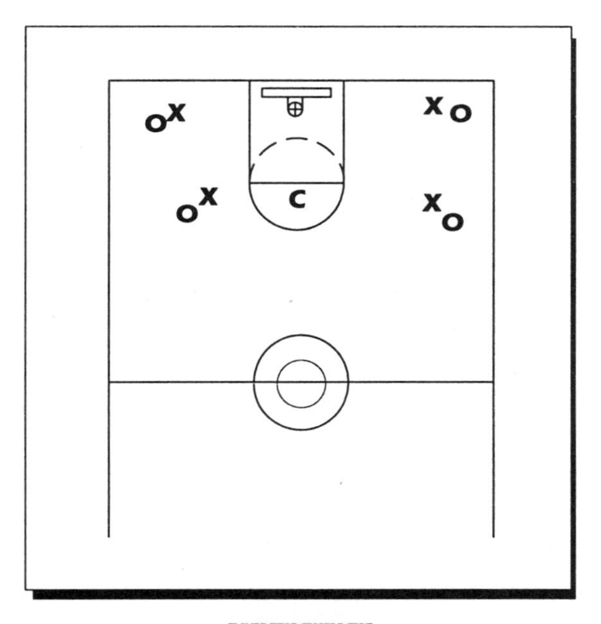

Drill #71: Combo Defense (6-on-4)

Objective: To teach pass denial under a variety of conditions.

Description: This drill involves four defensive players, four offensive players, and two coaches. Position the four offensive players in a shell around the half court. The four defensive players assume a good, tight defensive position on their respective offensive player. Two coaches begin the drill in the two corners of the half court. The offensive players move anywhere they want in an attempt to create a favorable passing lane from the corners. Variations on this drill can include any or all of the following: (1) limit the number of passes the offense may take; (2) allow or deny cuts by the offensive team; (3) require that each play must start with a screen and roll by the offense; and (4) designate one offensive player as the shooter. Each of these variations creates different situations for the defense. On the signal to "change" from one of the coaches, the offense and defense switch assignments.

Coaching Point:

- The primary principles of man-to-man defense should be emphasized, including pressure on the ball at all times, deny-defense one pass from the ball, and help-defense two passes from the ball.

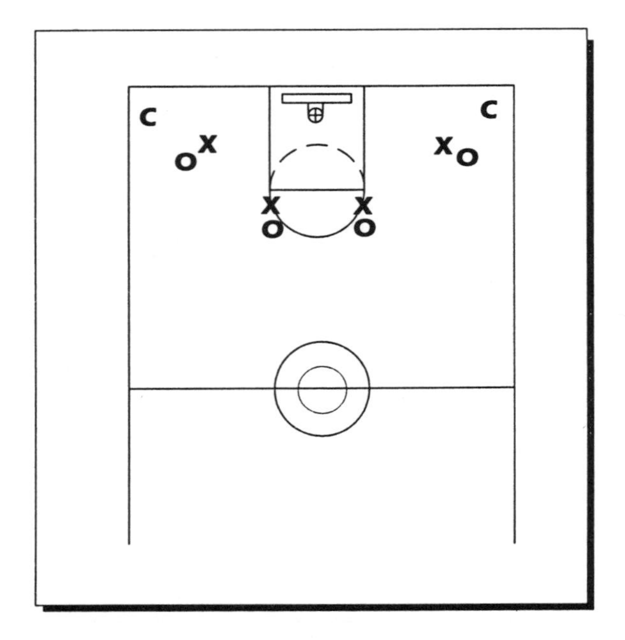

Drill #72: Combo Defense (5-on-5)

Objective: To teach pass denial under a variety of conditions.

Description: The drill involves five offensive and five defensive players. Position four offensive players in a shell around the half court similar to the previous drill and add the fifth offensive player in the center of the free throw lane. Five defensive players assume a good, tight defensive position on their respective offensive player. The offensive players move anywhere they want in an attempt to create a favorable passing lane from their teammates. Variations on this drill can include any or all of the following: (1) limit the number of passes the offense may take; (2) allow or deny cuts by the offensive team; (3) require that each play must start with a screen and roll by the offense; (4) and designate one offensive player as the shooter. Each of these variations creates different situations for the defense. On the signal to "change" from the coach, the offense and defense switch assignments. The drill can be used to set up competitions between "teams" of players using whatever criteria the coach deems appropriate, e.g., length of time the defense prevented the offense from shooting, the number of passes needed to get an open shot, etc.

Coaching Point:

- The primary principles of man-to-man defense should be emphasized, including pressure on the ball at all times, deny-defense one pass from the ball, and help-defense two passes from the ball.

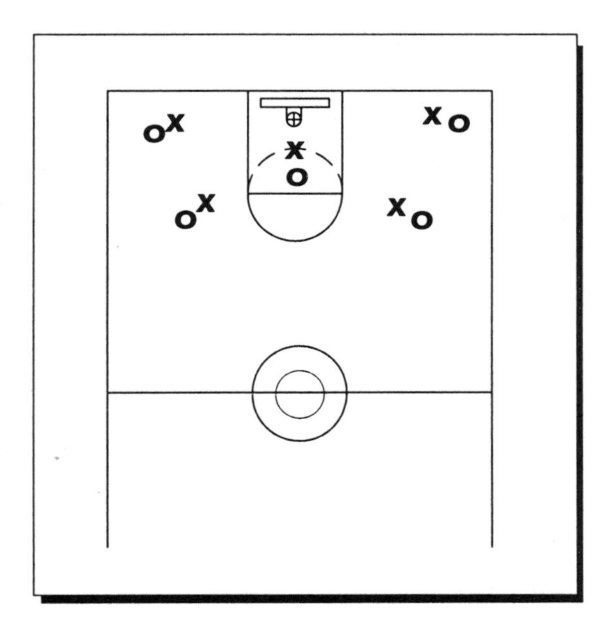

Drill #73: Rotation Drill

Objective: To improve the ability of two defensive players to rotate from strongside defense to weakside defense to helpside defense.

Description: Two offensive players are positioned in a baseline position on opposite sides of the court outside the free throw lane, while the third offensive player is positioned near the elbow of the lane with a basketball. The coach assumes a position where a guard would play in the area opposite the third offensive player. The two defensive players assume good defensive positions on the baseline player and the third offensive player on the side of the court opposite the coach. The drill starts with a pass to the coach. On the pass, the two defenders move off their respective players and assume good weakside defense. They maintain eye contact with their offensive player and the ball. The pass from the coach to the baseline offensive player triggers the helpside rotation of the two defensive players. The defensive player nearest the baseline moves immediately to the ball to prevent the drive, while the other defensive player drops down through the lane to prevent the cross-court pass. The ball is then reversed, and the defense adjusts accordingly.

Coaching Points:

- The defensive players work and rotate as a team to ensure that they enforce the highest level possible of defensive pressure, coverage and help to other teammates.
- Each player has an assigned task in strongside, weakside and helpside defense that should be explained as it relates to the larger concept of total team defense.

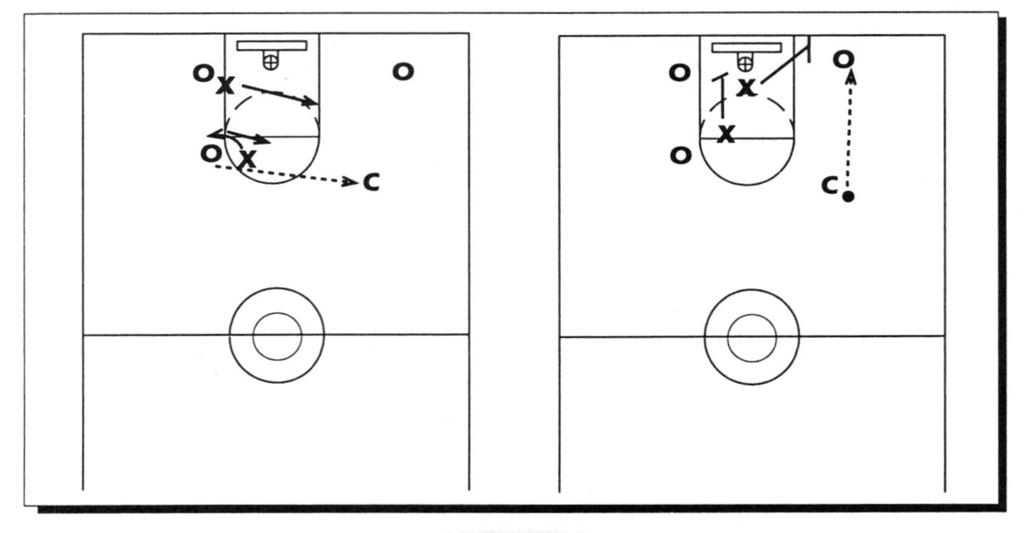

Drill #74: Composite Cutting

Objective: To teach denial of the pass from the wing to several different post positions.

Description: The drill involves two offensive players ("P" and "O") and a defender ("X"). One of the offensive players (P) serves as a passer and assumes a high wing position. The other offensive player (O) assumes a position at the baseline corner of the lane on the same side as the passer. This player utilizes three basic movements in an attempt to present a good passing lane for the passer. The first cut is directly to the corner of the court; the second is across the lane on the baseline and then diagonally across the lane to the corner nearest to the passer; while the third is down the side of the free throw lane back to the starting position. The defensive player works on denying the passing lanes to the three points of possible pass reception: (1) the corner of the court; (2) the elbow of the lane; and (3) the side of the lane closest to the passer. She must maintain good foot and hand position to deny the passing lane throughout the entire movement pattern of the offensive player. Seeing both the offensive player and the ball is critical. Moving two steps for each step taken by the offensive player allows the defensive player to be in a proper pass denial position at all times.

Coaching Points:

- The ability to maintain a good denial position under a variety of different situations should be emphasized.
- Maintaining simultaneous eye contact with the ball and the offensive player should be emphasized.

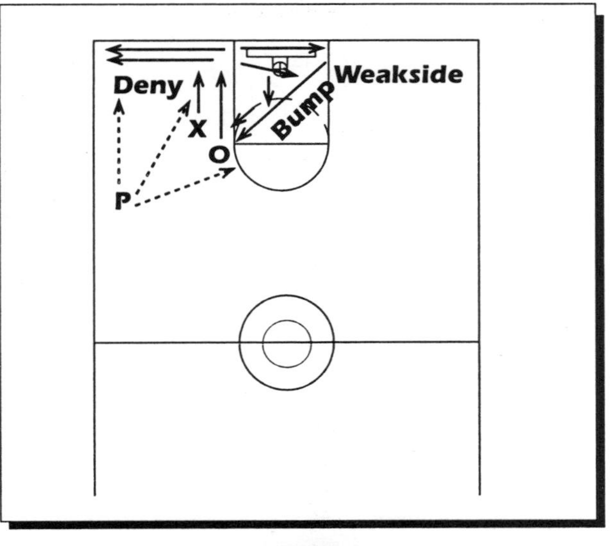

Drill #75: Cutting the Flash

Objective: To defend against cutter from the weak side to the ball.

Description: The drill involves two offensive players ("P" and "O") and one defensive player ("X"). One of the offensive players (P) is positioned on the wing with a basketball. The other offensive player (O) begins from a low position on the side opposite the player with the ball. The defensive player (X) assumes a good defensive position approximately in the center of the free throw lane. The defender maintains simultaneous eye contact on both the offensive player and the basketball. The offensive player (O) attempts to receive a pass from "P" at the elbow of the lane closest to the passer. The defensive player must defend two possible paths for "O" to receive the ball: (1) the cut directly from the original starting position diagonally across the lane to the "elbow" of the lane, and (2) the fake to the elbow of the lane and the cut directly across the lane to the midpost position closest to the passer.

Coaching Points:

- This drill should stress denying the pass to the offensive team's desired spot. Forcing the offensive player away from the elbow of the key and more toward the top of the free throw circle is disruptive to the offensive team's game plan.

- Adjusting the defensive position to the offensive player's cut should also be emphasized. When denied access to the elbow of the lane, the offensive player must adjust to another desirable spot, and the defensive player should learn to adjust and deny this spot in the same manner.

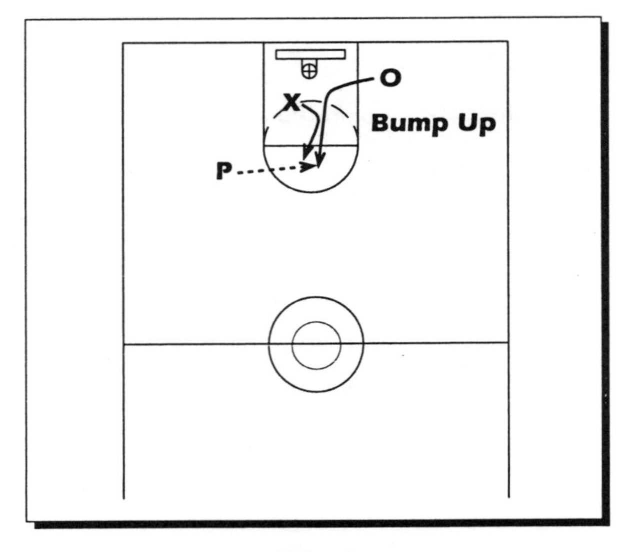

MAN-TO-MAN DEFENSIVE DRILLS

Drill #76: One-on-One

Objective: To teach one-on-one defense.

Description: Divide the team into four groups: two offensive groups and two defensive groups. The offensive groups line up at mid-court with one group facing each basket. The two defensive groups lineup on the baseline (out of bounds) facing the center court area. The first person in each defensive line goes to the mid-court area and assumes a good defensive position. The first person in the offensive line begins with a basketball and attempts to drive the length of the half court for a lay-up against the efforts of a defender. Each player takes their turn and switches lines upon completion of their turn.

Coaching Points:

- This drill should emphasize maintaining proper foot position and beating the offensive player to the desired spot on the floor as a way to force the offensive player to a position outside the lane.

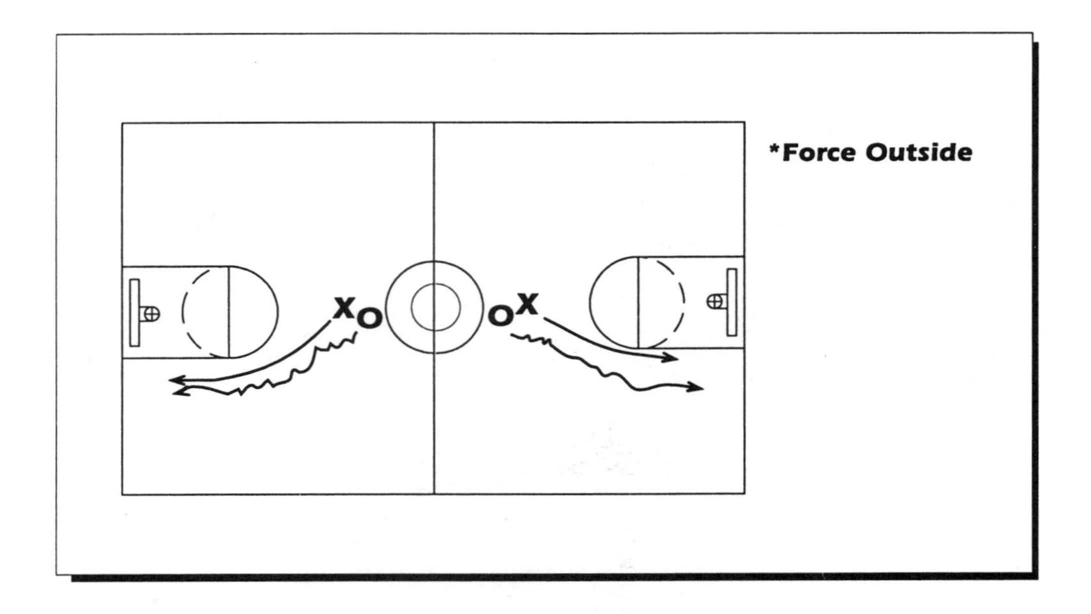

Drill #77: Shell-Four-on-Four

Objective: To teach the fundamentals and techniques of man-to-man defense.

Description: Position the four offensive players in a "shell" around the half court area with two players near the elbows and the other two in the corners approximately half way between the free throw lane and the sideline. The four defensive players should assume a good, tight defensive position on their respective offensive player. The offense tries to score, while the defense tries to stop them from scoring. Variations on this drill can include any or all of the following: (1) limit the number of passes the offense may take; (2) allow or deny cuts by the offensive team; (3) require that each play must start with a screen and roll by the offense; (4) and designate one offensive player as the shooter. Each of these variations creates different situations for the defense. On the signal to "change" from the coach, the offense and defense switch assignments.

Coaching Points:

- The primary principles of man-to-man defense should be emphasized, including pressure on the ball at all times, deny-defense one pass from the ball, and help-defense two passes from the ball.

- Variety can be incorporated into the drill by either adding a fifth offensive player (thereby forcing the defense to contend with a 5-on-4 situation) or positioning two coaches in the two corners of the court and having them assist the offense by serving as primary passers only.

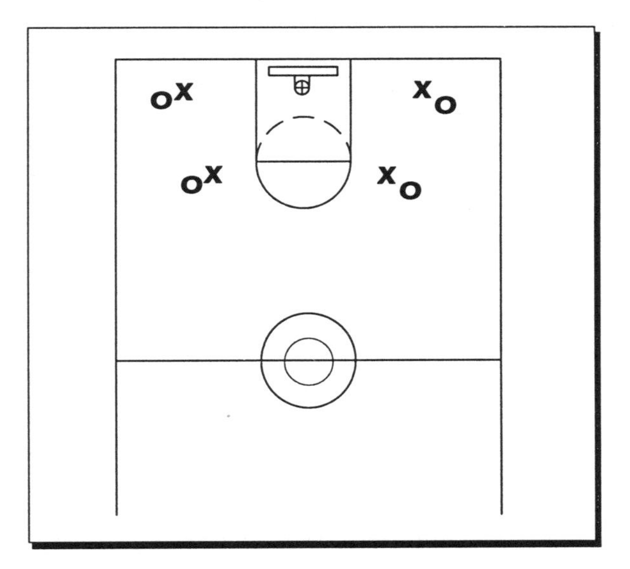

Drill #78: Double-Team Trap

Objective: To teach the double-team trap and anticipating the pass.

Description: Position three offensive players in a triangular arrangement with one at the top of the key and one on each side of the free throw lane approximately five feet outside the low block. Position three defensive players so that two are above the free throw line in the free throw circle. The third defensive player is located in the middle of the free throw lane directly in front of the basket. The ball begins in the hands of the player at the top of the key. None of the offensive players may move from their spots on the floor. The drill begins with the ball being passed from the top of the key to one of the low block area players. The closest defender and the player in the lane immediately double team the ball, while the third defender splits the difference between the two offensive players. The third defensive player must be ready to shoot the gap and steal or deflect a pass. The offense keeps the ball until the defense steals or deflects three passes. Then, six new players are rotated into the drill.

Coaching Points:

- Maintaining proper foot/body position and avoiding reaching with the hands should be emphasized.

- Learning how to split the difference between two offensive players and anticipate a pass will result in more deflections and steals for the defense.

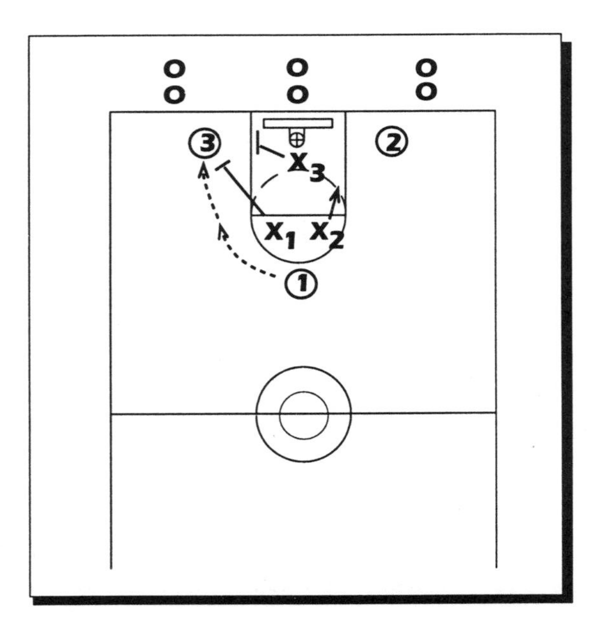

Drill: #79: Shooting the Gap

Objective: To teach the defender to read the offensive passer and to steal the ball.

Description: The drill involves six players—three on offense and three on defense. Place the three offensive players in a triangle with one player in the corner, one player in the free throw lane near the low block and the third player slightly above the wing on the same side of the floor. The remainder of the team forms a single line outside the court near the corner position. The three defenders used in this drill should assume positions so that two are double-teaming the corner player, while the other defender should be between the other two offensive players. Neither of these two offensive players may move to receive the pass from the corner. The coach begins the drill by passing the ball to the corner player. Whether or not the corner player can dribble is the option of the coach. The two defenders double team the corner player, while the third player attempts to steal or deflect the pass. The corner player is limited to using either a bounce pass or a direct pass.

Coaching Points:

- This drill puts more pressure on the one defender charged with deflecting or stealing the pass. She should practice learning the gap, reading the passer, and knowing the proper defensive position.

- Good double team pressure, including hands in the passing lanes, should also be emphasized.

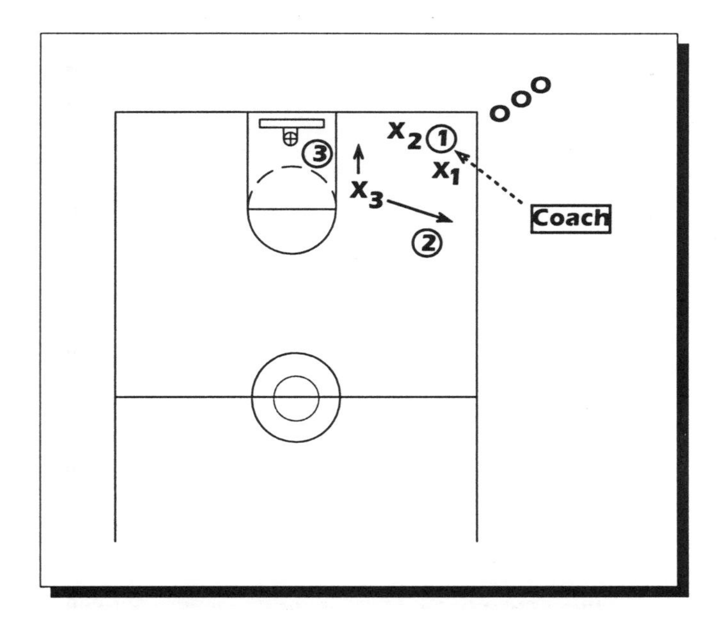

Drill #80: Proper Dive

Objective: To teach defense on the strong side of the ball.

Description: This 3-on-3 drill involves three offensive and three defensive players. The three offensive players are positioned on one side of the half court. One offensive player is in the corner, one offensive player is on the low block and the other offensive player is in the guard position. The three defensive players assume good defensive positions on their respective offensive players. The guard begins the drill with the basketball. She is not permitted to dribble and is not allowed to use a lob pass to get the ball to either the post position or the corner. The offensive players without the ball may move in any direction and may use screens to make themselves available for an entry pass from the guard. It is the defense's responsibility to deny this pass through proper body position depending on the location of the ball. If the ball penetrates to the corner position, the corner defender immediately closes off the baseline drive or the pass. The post defender then rotates from highside denial to lowside denial. The player defending the guard "dives" to the low post area to force the pass from the corner back outside.

Coaching Point:

- This drill should stress first denying the pass into the low post, then denying the pass into the corner. If the pass into the corner is completed, the guard assists the post defender in preventing the entry pass into the low post by diving down and forcing the ball back out to the guard.

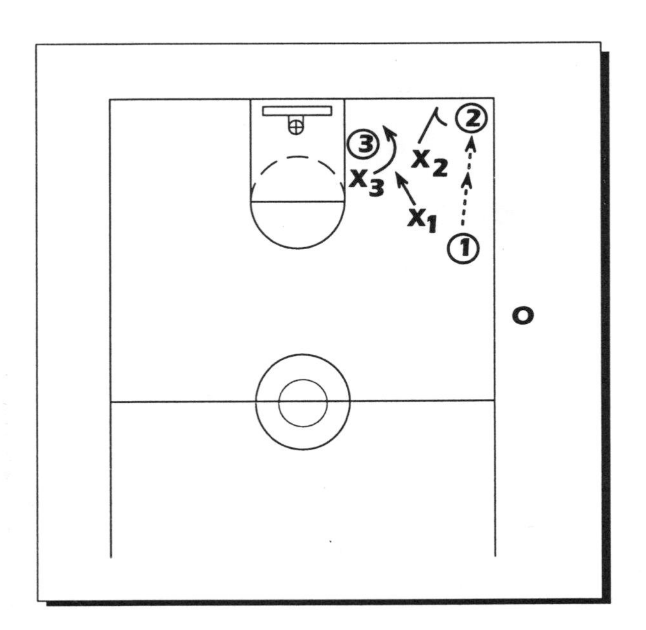

CHAPTER 11

ZONE DEFENSE DRILLS

Drill #81: Trap, Hedge, and Switch

Objective: To teach the principles of the full-court zone press.

Description: The drill involves 12 players—six on offense and six on defense. The full court is divided into three zones: a middle zone the width of the free throw lane that extends the full length of the court, and the two zones which consist of the outer one-third on each side of the lane. Each zone involves four players who must stay within their respective zone. Three offensive players (one per zone) are positioned on the baseline, each with a basketball. The other three offensive players are positioned on the half court line. Three defenders (one per zone) are positioned on the baseline facing the offensive players who have a basketball. The three other defenders are positioned near, but not closely guarding, the three offensive players near the half-court line. The drill can involve three separate scenarios: The players in all three zones can be doing the same thing, the players in all three zones can be doing different things, or the choice of what fundamentals to work on can be left to the defenders. The drill begins with the baseline offensive players penetrating up the court using the dribble. The first defender and her teammate at half-court permit the ball to advance until they decide to trap the player utilizing the double-team. They then attempt to prevent the pass to half-court and steal the ball if possible. This is illustrated in the top zone of diagram #81. The middle zone of diagram #81 illustrates the hedge. As the player advances via the dribble, the half-court defender hedges toward her and fakes the trap. As the dribbler picks the ball up to pass to the half-court line, the defender retreats and attempts to steal the pass. The final principle is shown at the bottom of diagram #81. As the ball advances, the baseline defender directs the dribbler toward the half-court line defender who has come up from her position. On the call of "switch", the half-court line defender charges the dribbler to stop the advance of the ball, while the baseline defender sprints to the passing lane in an attempt to deflect or steal the ball.

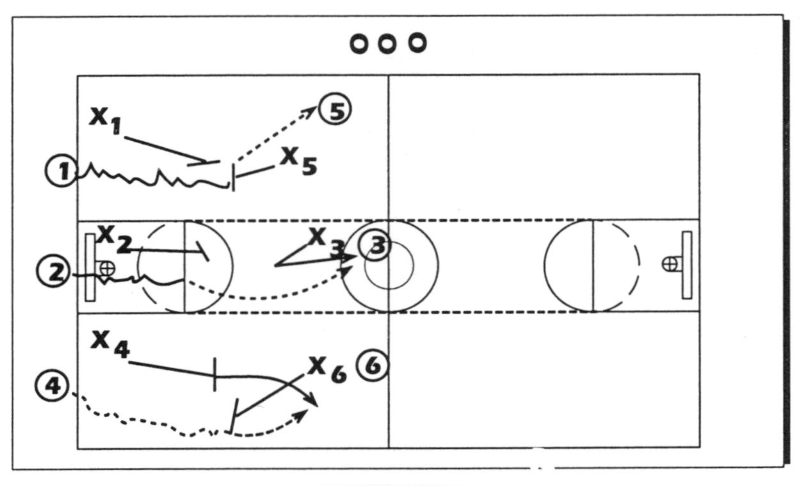

Drill #82: Eight-on-Four

Objective: To teach match-up zone fundamentals and techniques.

Description: The drill involves eight offensive and four defensive players. Seven of the offensive players are positioned as follows—four across the baseline (one in each corner and one on each low block), one at each of the elbows of the lane, and one on the free throw line. The four defensive players form a box inside the free throw lane. The coach begins the drill with the basketball at the top of the key. The initial pass must go from the coach to any of the four offensive players on the baseline. If the pass goes to the corner (the pass to the inside two baseline players should be easy enough to deny), the strongside low block player applies defensive pressure on the ball; the weakside low block defender slides around the low block offensive player and fronts her; the strongside guard covers the high post area and prevents the return pass to the top of the key; and the weakside guard drops to the middle to cover cuts from the weakside. While the ball is in the corner, the player who has received the pass may only pass to the three closest players to her and may not use a lob pass over the zone. She may also drive to the basket and shoot. If a drive to the baseline is attempted, the low block defenders should execute a double-team trap, while the weakside guard should slide down to the low block to defend against the penetration pass. If the corner player drives toward the basket away from the baseline the strongside guard and strongside low block player should execute a double-team, while the weakside guard should slide to cover the high post area. The drill begins again when the pass is returned to the coach at the top of the key.

Coaching Point:

- This drill should stress sliding to adjust to changing positions by the offense.

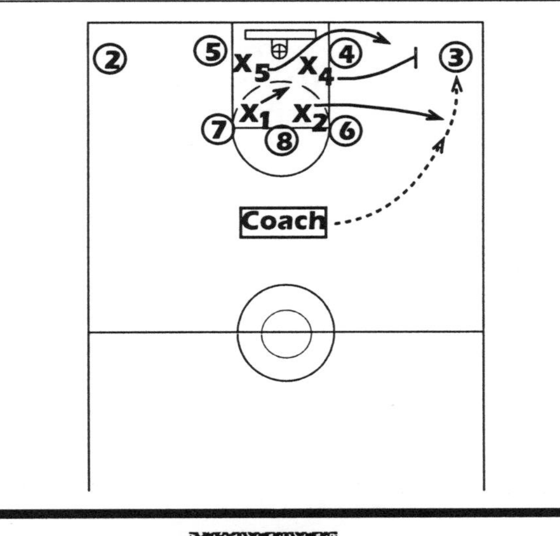

Drill #83: Bull-in-Ring-Trap

Objective: To teach trapping techniques and fundamentals.

Description: Three defensive players are needed for this drill. The remaining members of the team are positioned in a circle that is sufficiently large to provide a defensive challenge for the three defenders to cover. Any player on the outer circle may begin the drill with the basketball. Whoever has the ball may not pass to a player adjacent to her. The three defensive players must double team the ball and, with the help of their teammates try to steal or deflect the pass. When a pass is completed to another player on the circle, the defenders rotate in accordance with the specific rules of the press the team is using. For example, the containing defender rotates, while the trapping defender stays. Any time a pass is deflected or stolen, the passer replaces the defender and the drill begins again.

Coaching Points:

- Besides teaching trapping techniques, this drill also provides the offense with the opportunity to deal with difficult passing lanes and pressure situations.

- For the offensive players, careful passing, faking, and stepping toward a pass when receiving it should be emphasized.

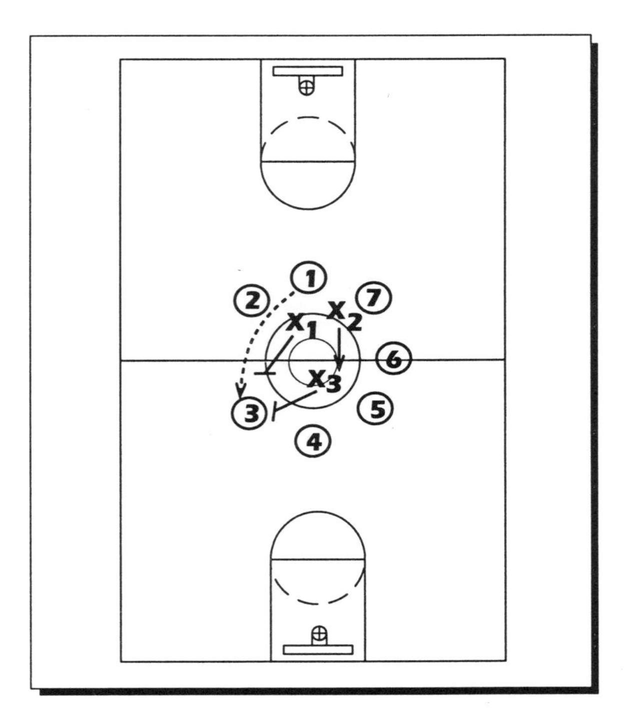

Drill #84: Channeling the Ball

Objective: To teach defenders in a zone defense to channel the ball to a favored position.

Description: The drill involves eight players—four on offense and four on defense. The four offensive players should be positioned with one in the high post area of the free throw line, one on each wing and one at the top of the key with a basketball. The four defensive players assume a match-up zone position with their respective offensive players, except that the point guard favors one side of the floor, creating a strongside and a weakside. The strongside wing adjusts into the passing lane between the top of the key and the wing. The weakside wing sags toward the middle. The coach may be positioned in either corner of the half-court. The point defender channels the ball to the favored wing. The strongside wing denies heavily, while the weakside wing invites the pass to her area. When the pass reaches the wing, the top defender denies the return pass to the top of the key, and the weakside wing pressures the ball. The original strongside wing drops to the middle of the free throw lane. The high post defender shades to the ball side of the post player. The wing is free to pass to the coach in the corner. In this case, the defense must adjust as follows: the post drops lower, the original strongside wing covers the low block area, and the original weakside wing denies the return pass to the wing. The offensive passer cuts through and the other two players rotate to fill the remaining two spots on the exterior of the offense.

Coaching Points:

- It should be stressed that the areas to which a team wants the ball channeled may differ according to their opponents' abilities or the defensive personnel available at any given time.

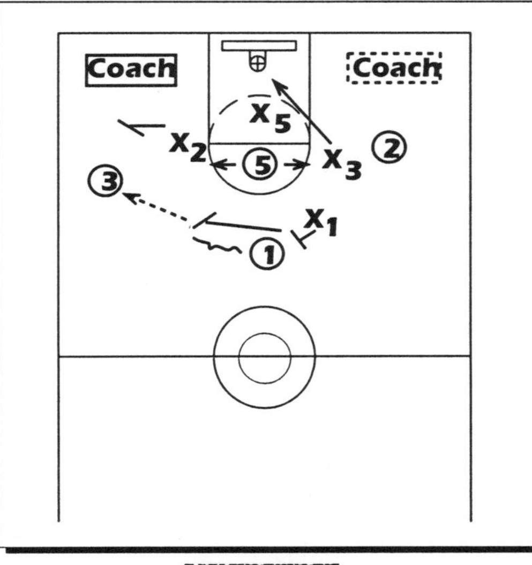

Drill #85: Cutters

Objective: To teach defenders in a zone defense to cover cutters.

Description: The drill involves eight players—four on offense and four on defense. The four offensive players assume the traditional two guard and two low wing positions. The four defensive players are in a box similar to the corners of a 2-1-2 zone. This configuration can be adjusted to fit a team's individual needs. The drill begins with the ball in the hands of one of the guards. The strongside defensive guard pressures the ball and the pass is made to the strongside wing. The strongside defensive forward goes out to challenge the ball as the offensive guard cuts through the zone. On the cut, the defense must adjust. The weakside forward slides across the free throw lane to the area in front of the basket. The weakside defensive guard then drops down to the middle of the free throw lane, and the strongside guard follows the cutter to the edge of the free throw lane. The next move by the defense is dictated by the cutter. If she goes across the lane, the strongside guard returns to the top corner of the zone, and the weakside forward releases back to her original low block area of the zone. If the cutter continues to the strongside corner, however, the strongside forward picks up the coverage and denies the pass from the low wing to the corner. The strongside guard then drops to cover the pass into the free throw lane. Any offensive player may pass and stay or pass and cut. Add shooting after the players have mastered the slides and coverages.

Coaching Point:

- Learning when to give the coverage to a teammate and communicating that action to her should be emphasized. Both verbal communication and repetitive actions can help ensure good zone coverage.

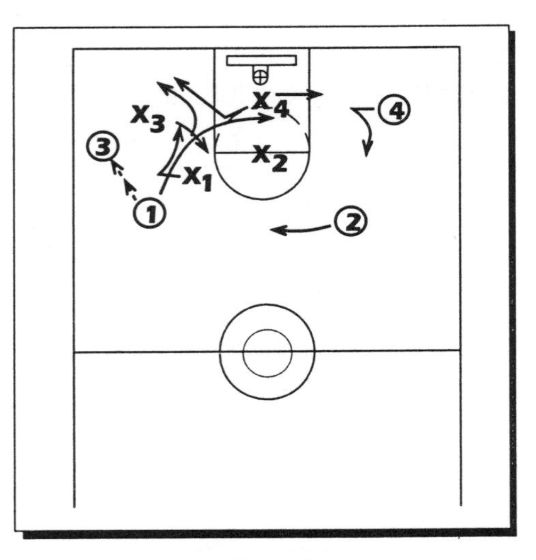

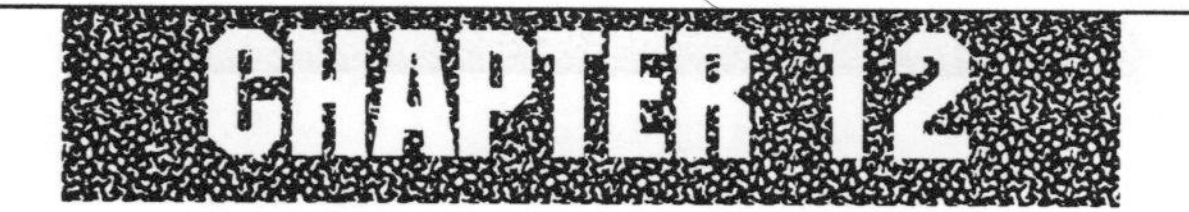

FAST BREAK DRILLS

Drill #86: Pass and Break

Objective: To teach making the lay up at the end of a fast break.

Description: Divide the team into two groups and position them on both sides of the full court near the half-court line, both facing the same basket. The line on the right side of the floor begins the drill with the first two to three players having a basketball. The first player in the line with the basketballs passes across the court to the first player in the other line. She takes one step toward the line she passed to and then breaks for the basket. The receiving player returns the pass for the execution of the lay up. No dribbling is allowed by either player. The players then return to the opposite line. Once the players become proficient in passing, a defender can be added to create a 2-on-1 situation.

Coaching Points:

- Since this drill requires the players to execute the passing and lay-up without dribbling the basketball, the emphasis should be on the timing of the passes and the footwork of the players involved.
- The player executing the lay-up should be able to receive the pass and lay the ball up without traveling, while the passer should time the pass and the location of the ball to enable the receiver to have the best opportunity to make the lay-up.

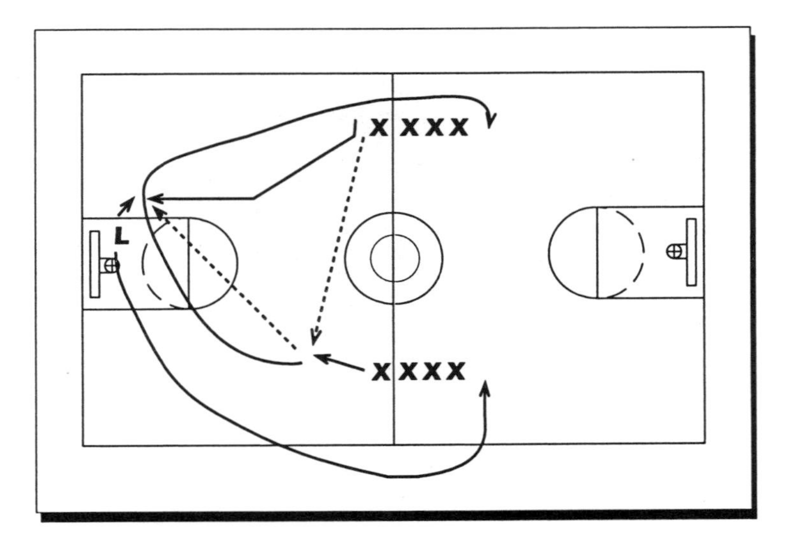

Drill #87: 2-on-1 Fast Break

Objective: To teach the execution of the 2-on-1 fast break.

Description: In this drill the team is divided into two offensive groups and positioned on one baseline off the court. One player is selected to begin the drill as the defensive player. She is positioned at the opposite end of the court at the free throw line. The drill begins with the first person in each of the two offensive lines moving down the court by exchanging passes. When they near the defensive player, they attempt to score by making a lay-up.

Coaching Points:

- All types of passes and dribble combinations can be attempted, but the offensive players should not become predictable in their attempts to score.
- The defensive players should focus on forcing the offense to commit to the first move. This allows the defense the best opportunity to either intercept the ball or delay the offense long enough for defensive help to arrive from down the court.

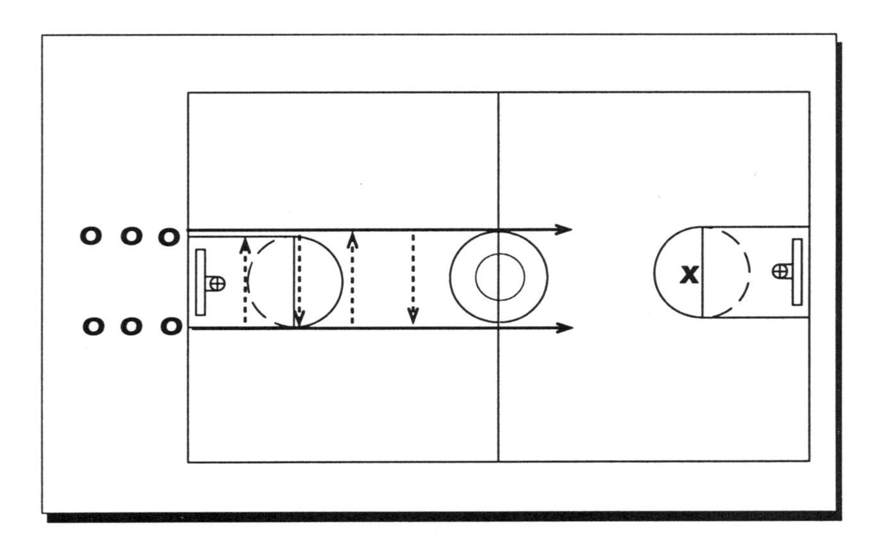

Drill #88: 3-on-2 Fast Break

Objective: To teach the 3-on-2 fast break and to improve conditioning.

Description: One pair of defensive players is positioned in tandem defense at both ends of the floor. At one end of the floor, two players are placed in the wing positions. These players are not involved in the initial 3-on-2 fast break. At the other end of the floor, three offensive players are spaced across the floor and ready to begin the initial 3-on-2 (the middle player has the basketball). Two additional wing offensive players are on either side of the floor. Neither is involved in either the first or the second 3-on-2 break situation. In all the 3-on-2 situations (either made or missed basket), the first defensive player to gain control of the basketball outlets the ball to the wing player and they fast break 3-on-2 to the opposite end. The remaining players then fill the voided spots and get ready for the next group. The drill is conducted in a continuous manner.

Coaching Points:

- The coach should stress maintaining a degree of solid defensive play against the 3-on-2 fast break. Coaches who wish to emphasize conditioning in this drill can allow this drill to continue for as long as the players fill the voided spots.

- This drill also mixes up the combinations of players involved in play so that the same groups are not dominating the drill and so that each player gets a better chance to "know" the other players on her team.

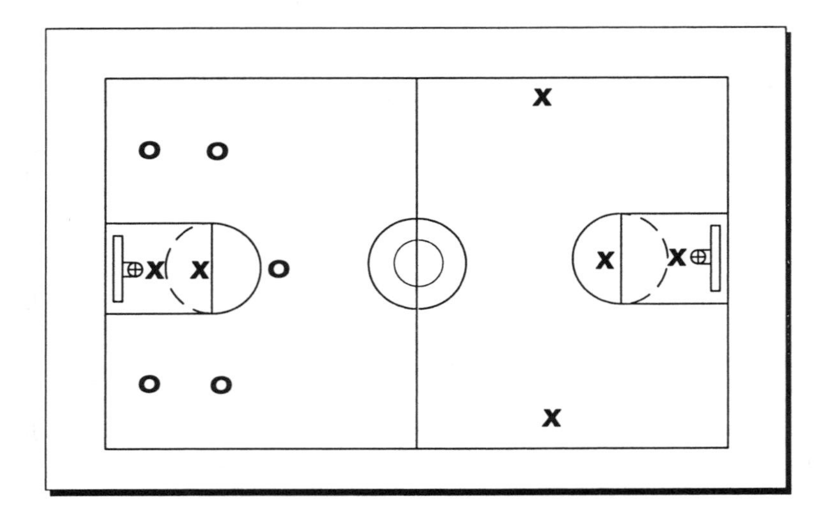

Drill #89: 3-on-3 Fast Break

Objective: To improve the ability to handle the basketball at full speed.

Description: This drill involves twelve players who are divided into two six-player teams. The drill begins with three offensive players spread out across the half-court line facing one end of the court. Two defensive players assume a defensive tandem position with their third defensive teammate positioned out of bounds at the half-court line. The drill begins with a 3-on-2 fast break. As the offense advances, the third defender sprints to the middle of the floor, and then attempts to catch up with the play. If the offense scores, their three offensive teammates at the half-court line start the drill over again by going on a 3-on-2 fast break against the same two original defenders. Once again, the third defender joins the drill once the offensive players have passed her position. On the other hand, if the defense secures the ball, the defense goes on offense at the other end of the floor as they fast break the length of the court. In this instance, the three offensive players who had been positioned off the court at the half-court line play defense. The first team to score ten baskets wins the game.

Coaching Points:

- This drill stresses 3-on-2 defense, catching up and transition, and also provides an opportunity to work on shot selection.

- The competitive aspect of this drill provides the teams with added incentive, but must be controlled by the coach or the play may get sloppy.

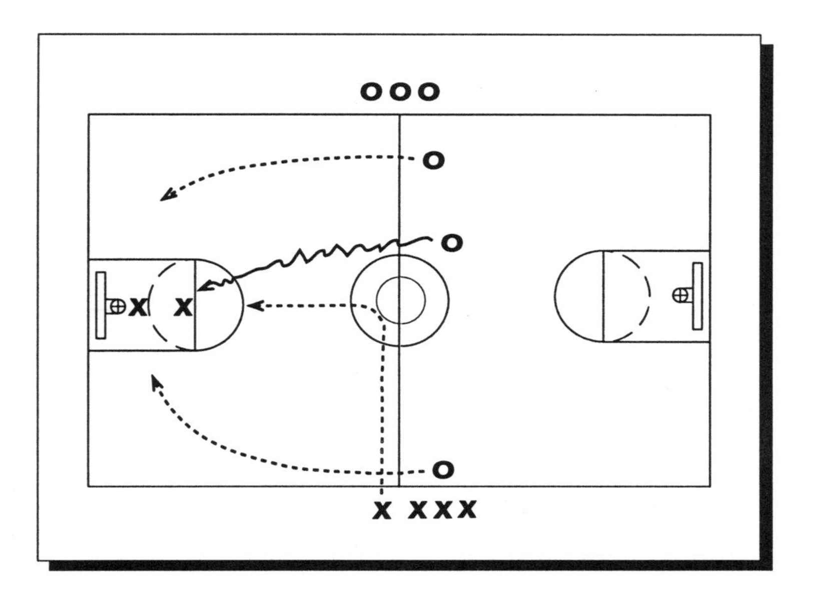

Drill #90: Go-for-It

Objective: To practice rebounding, outlet passing and fast break movements.

Description: Divide the team into four groups and position two of the lines on both sides of the free throw lane facing the basket and the other two groups in the wing areas on both sides of the floor. The coach begins the drill with a basketball on the free throw line. The coach shoots and misses a free throw. The first two players in each of the free throw lane lines battle for the rebound. The player who secures the rebound outlets the ball to the first player in the closest wing area line to begin the fast break. The opposite wing player breaks to the middle to receive the pass from the wing and fill the middle lane of the fast break. The rebounder who did not get the rebound fills the third lane and the three players go the length of the floor for the lay up.

Coaching Points:

- Rebounders should work on their aggressiveness, anticipation, and general rebounding techniques.
- Players can also practice making and receiving the outlet pass, breaking to the middle, dribbling, and filling the third lane of the fast break.

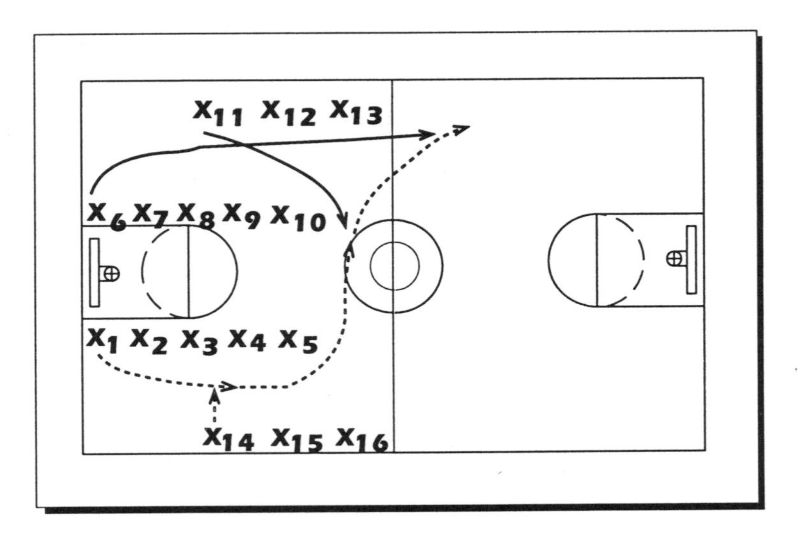

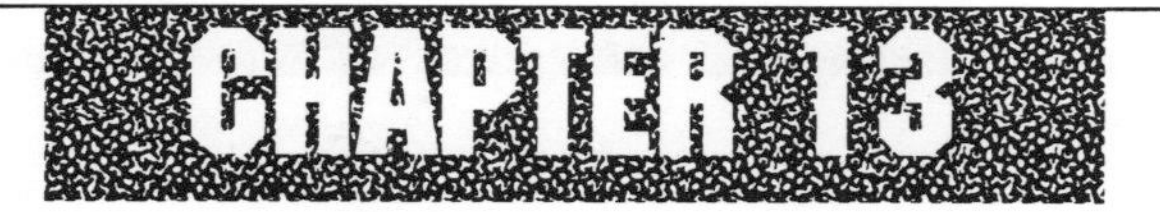

QUICKNESS AND REACTION DRILLS

Drill #91: Quick Response

Objective: To improve quickness and reaction time.

Description: This drill is a series of three drills involving the use of a wall to work on improving reaction time. In the first part of the drill, a player (standing approximately five away from a wall) takes two balls and bounces/catches them off the wall one at a time. The pass and the catch should be with two hands and from the chest. This action is somewhat similar to juggling. In the second part of the drill, a player (standing approximately five feet from a wall with her back to the wall) throws the ball directly back over her head to the wall. The player then jumps, turns and catches the ball in front of her. The player should be facing the wall when she catches the ball. In the third part of the drill, a player (standing approximately five feet from and facing the wall) has a partner from behind her throw a ball off the wall. The player should catch the ball before it hits the floor. Immediately after catching the ball, the player should flip it over her shoulder to the passer for the next toss.

Coaching Points:

- The emphasis should be on developing each player's reaction time to her maximum potential.
- As players progress, decreasing the distance between the player and the wall will increase the difficulty of the drill.

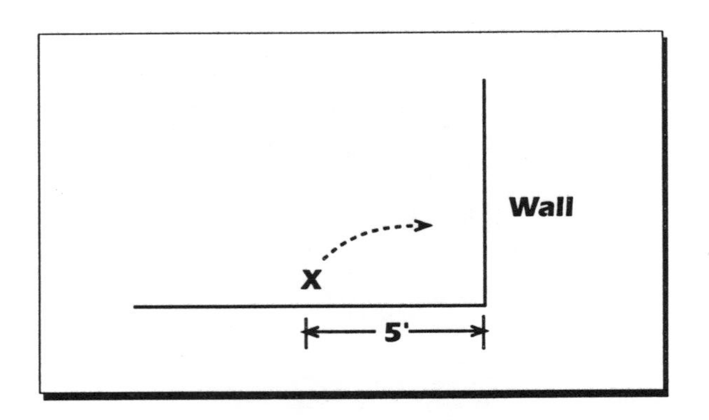

Drill #92: Straddle the Line

Objective: To enhance footwork, quickness, and footspeed.

Description: This drill is a series of three drills in one. The drill should last approximately 45 seconds and be divided equally between the three segments. In all parts of the drill the players begin in a low, good defensive position. Segment 1: With the players straddling a line the players begin by moving their legs to a crossed position with the right leg crossed over their left without stepping on the line. The player then returns to the straddling the line position and crosses the left leg over the right. Again, this action is done without stepping on the line. The player then returns to the starting position and begins the drill again. Segment 2: With both feet together, the players jump from one side of the line to the other without touching the line. Segment 3: With the players straddling the line the players make 180 degree jump turns without touching the line. The speed of the segments increases as the players become more proficient.

Coaching Points:

- Timing the number of repetitions and keeping an on-going record on the players' progress can provide them with excellent feedback of how they are doing.

- The goal of every player should be to get better and faster at performing these segments because a player's performance on such events translates directly into improved defensive skill and abilities.

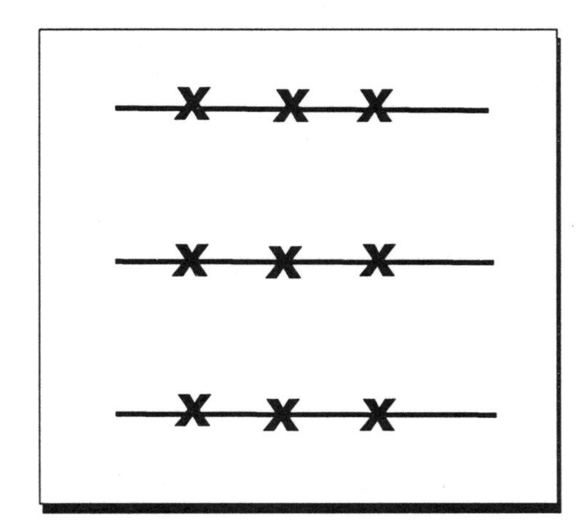

Drill #93: Mirror Defense

Objective: To develop quickness, reaction time and foot speed.

Description: Pair the players according to speed and size. The players face each other. One player is designated as the offensive player, while the other is designated as the defensive player. The players must operate laterally between the side line of the full court and the sideline of the free throw lane extended. The forward and backward movement of the pair is limited by the space available and the number of pairs you have working at the same time. The offensive player begins with a ball and moves in any direction possible within the designated area to break free of the defensive player. Maintaining a good defensive position without using her hands, the defensive player shadows the offensive player.

Coaching Points:

- The offensive player should try a variety of moves to make the defender work as hard as possible.

- The defensive player should concentrate on the footwork involved in beating the offense to a desirable spot on the floor. Use of the hands to check the progress of the offensive player is strictly prohibited.

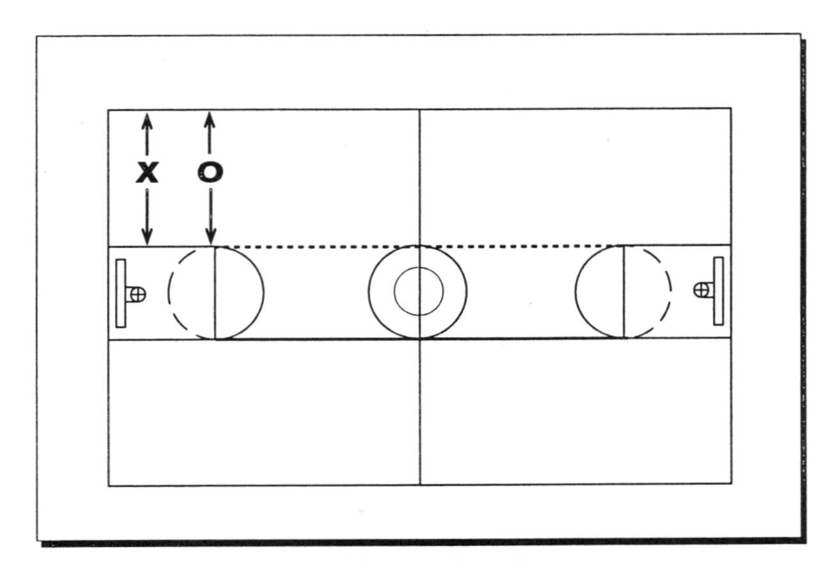

Drill #94: Advance and Defend

Objective: To enhance foot speed and improve conditioning.

Description: In this drill, the full court is divided into three zones. The middle zone involves an area which is the width of the free throw lane and extends the full length of the court. The other two zones consist of the outer area on each side of the free throw lane to the sideline. Each pair of players must stay within their respective zone. Three offensive players (one per zone) are positioned on the baseline, each having a basketball. Three defensive players (one per zone) are positioned just inside the baseline facing the offensive players. The drill begins with the offensive players advancing the ball down the floor against the defense. The defensive player must cut off the advance of the offensive player she is guarding and make her reverse direction. The advancing and turning motion of the play continues the full length of the court.

Coaching Points:

- The defensive slides should be done in a good defensive position. If the offensive player gets ahead of the defense, she should wait for her defender to catch up and resume good defensive play.

- The defender may not check the progress of the offensive player by using her hands at any time.

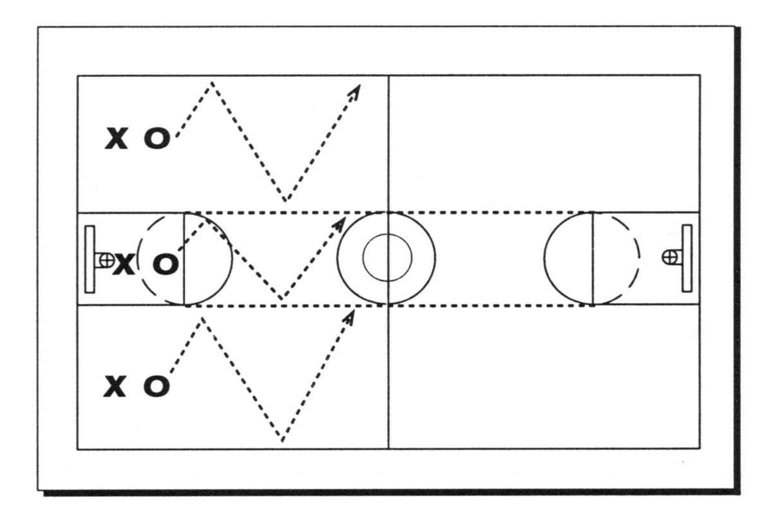

Drill #95: Foot Fire

Objective: To increase foot movement and quickness.

Description: The player stands facing the coach. On a given signal, the player alternates, lifting each foot as quickly as possible. Each player participates in the drill for a period of thirty seconds. This drill can be used with as few as one player or as many as the entire team. The object of the drill is to increase the foot movement and quickness of each player.

Coaching Point:

- The player should assume a good defensive position with her hands in a ready-to-guard position and her knees bent, and maintain a proper defensive position throughout the duration of the drill.

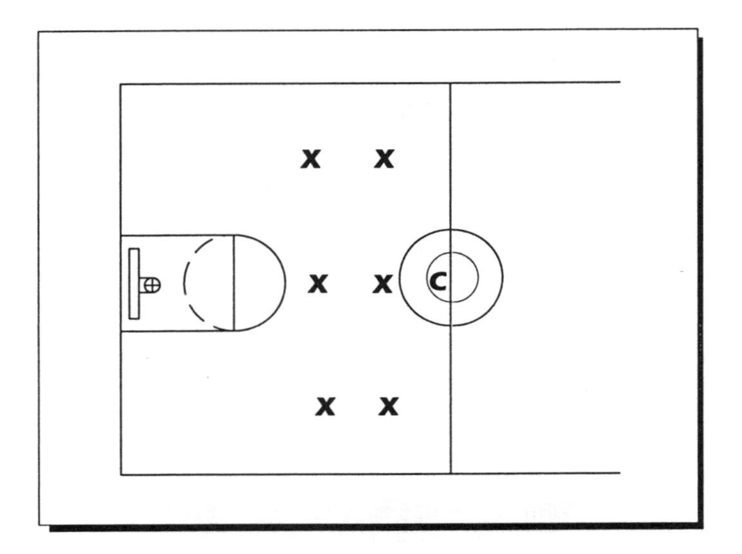

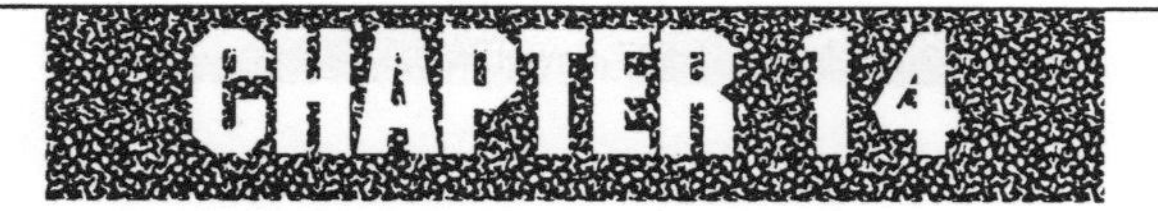

CONDITIONING DRILLS

Drill #96: Slide to the Side

Objective: To improve stamina and enhance the ability to move side-to-side.

Description: Each player, one at a time, assumes a good defensive position on the baseline directly under the basket. The coach begins the drill while standing on the free throw line with two basketballs. The coach rolls one of the basketballs to the right of the player on the baseline. The player, utilizing a good defensive slide, moves over, picks up the ball and makes a good two-handed chest pass back to the coach. The coach then rolls the second ball to the players' left as she picks up the first ball. The speed of the ball and the distance to the right or left increases as the drill progresses until the player is going sideline to sideline. If the ball passes the baseline without the player picking it up, the drill begins again.

Coaching Points:

- Emphasis should be on maintaining a proper defensive position during the slides as the drill progresses.

- This drill is also an excellent conditioning drill and may be performed while other players are shooting free throws.

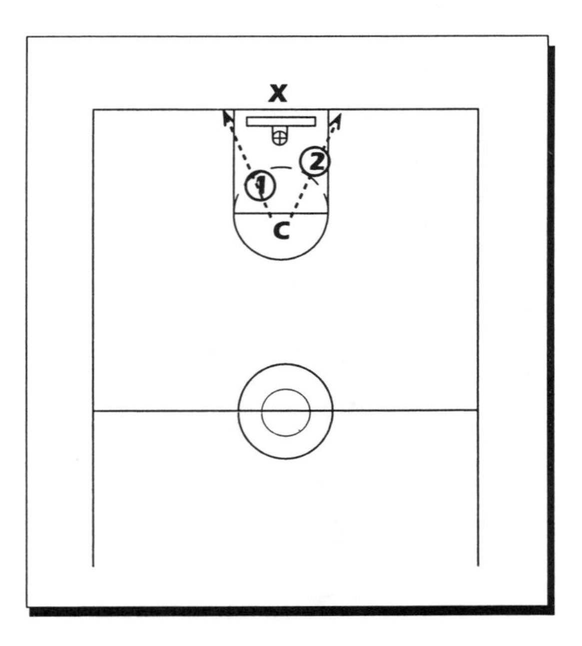

Drill #97 : Four-on-the-Go

Objective: To improve physical conditioning and to practice shooting lay-ups at full speed.

Description: Divide the team into four groups and position them at each of the four 28-foot marks on the full court. One player begins the drill by bouncing the ball off the backboard and making the rebound. She makes an outlet pass to the first player in the line on her side of the court while moving in a counterclockwise direction. The player breaks down the court and receives a return pass from the player in the first line who received the initial pass. The player continues down the court and passes to the first player in the second line (positioned at the opposite end 28-foot mark). She continues down the court, receives a return pass from the second line player, and shoots a lay-up at full speed. The player rebounds the ball and repeats the process down the opposite side of the court. The players who function as passers rotate to the end of the next line, while the shooter goes to the end of the first passing line. More than one player may be going through the drill at one time.

Coaching Points:

- While this is primarily a full-speed conditioning drill which emphasizes constant movement at all times, it should also stress learning to shoot lay-ups at full speed and make accurate passes to a player on the move.

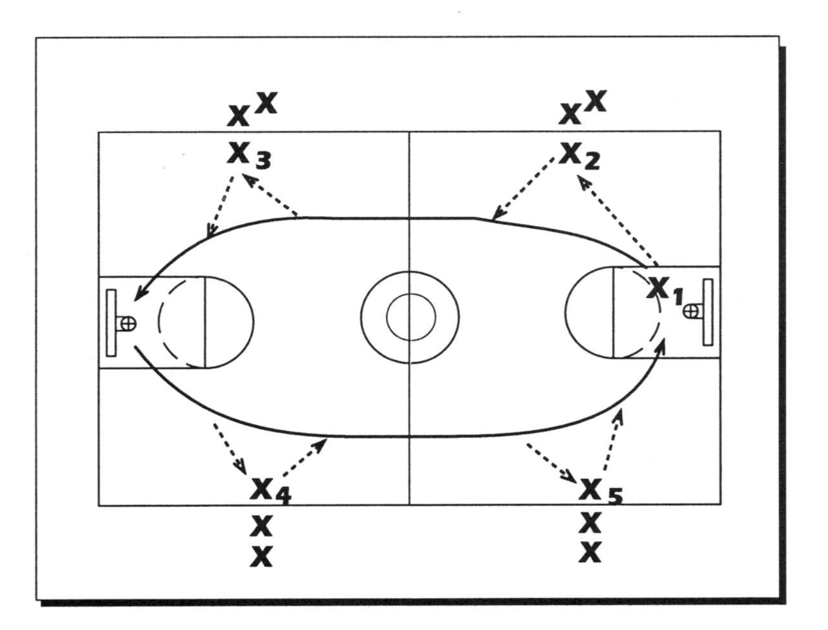

Drill #98: One-on-One-Conditioning

Objective: To enhance conditioning; to develop aggressiveness; to practice playing in a competitive 1-on-1 situation.

Description: Divide the team into front court and back court players. Put one group at one end of the court on the baseline and the other group on the opposite baseline. Two players participate in the drill at each end of the floor. The drill begins when the coach at each end rolls a ball from under the basket toward the center of the court. The two players sprint after the basketball. When one recovers the loose ball, the coach yells a number that corresponds with one of the three baskets in that end of the court. The play continues 1-on-1 at that basket until one of the players scores. There are no boundaries in the drill, and there is no stoppage of play because of fouls. Aggressive play should be stressed.

Coaching Points:

- Reaction to the ball and the need to immediately get into a proper offensive/defensive position after the coach designates the basket should be emphasized.
- Playing tough 1-on-1 defense without help from teammates will help to increase the player's defensive intensity.
- Having players begin with their backs to the playing floor and rolling the ball in different areas of the half-court can add variety to the drill.

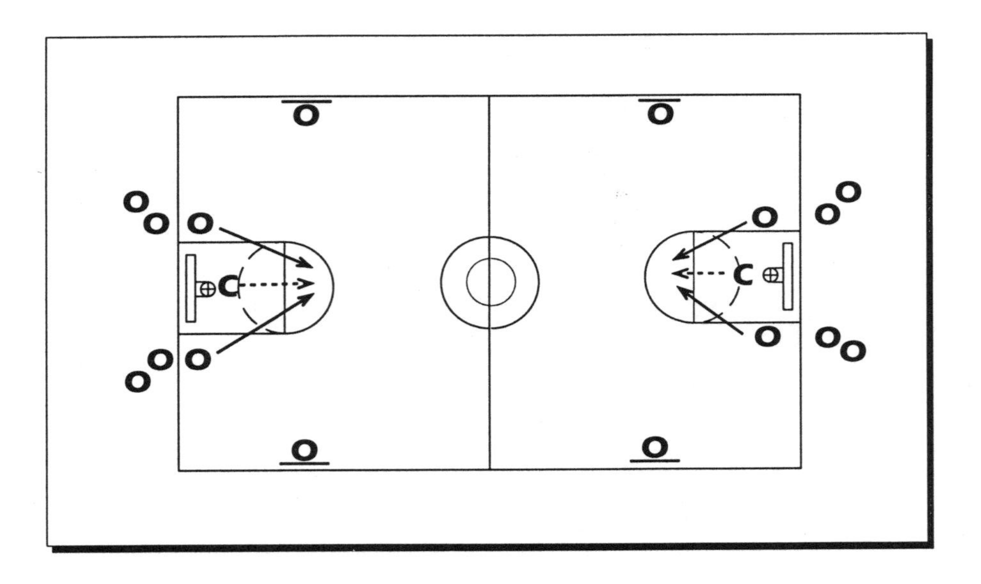

Drill #99: Sprint and Go

Objective: To improve conditioning and to practice passing, shooting and cutting.

Description: Divide the team into three groups and position them on the baseline, spaced equally across the entire width of the floor. The first player in the middle line begins the drill by passing the ball to the first person in either of the other two lines. This pass should be completed when the player is somewhere in the vicinity of the free throw line extended or the 28-foot mark. The first player in the third line sprints straight down the floor until she reaches the division line. At that point, she cuts directly for the basket and receives a pass diagonally across the floor. This pass should be received in the vicinity of the opposite end free throw line. The original passer sprints the length of the floor, rebounds the made lay-up and outlets the ball to the shooter in the vicinity of the free throw line extended or the 28-foot mark. The receiver of the first outlet pass sprints the floor to the opposite free throw line, then turns down the other side of the floor to receive the second long pass and shoot the second lay up.

Coaching Points:

- This drill should stress that both the outlet pass and the long diagonal pass must be accurate for the player on the move to receive the pass in stride and handle it properly.

- Players should practice throwing a baseball pass with a minimum of side spin to keep the ball from curving as it travels.

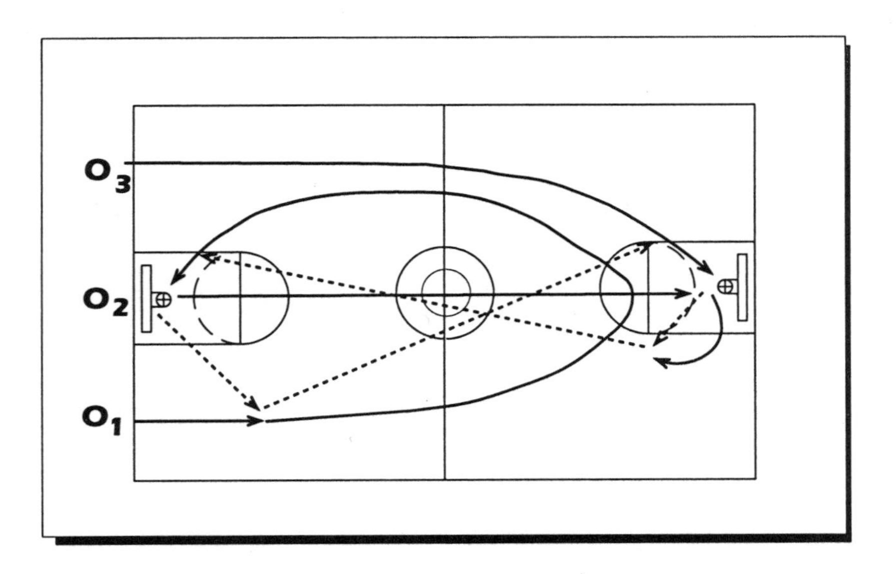

Drill #100: Anything Goes

Objective: To improve conditioning; to develop aggressiveness; to practice transition.

Description: This drill involves dividing the teams into groups of two players in such a way that all the "teams" are as evenly matched in skill level as possible. The drill is played on a full court with four side baskets if possible. The two-on-two play begins with a jump ball at the center circle. The team that controls the tap can score at any of the six baskets on the court. The made basket can be retrieved by either of the two teams that can, in turn, score at any of the baskets on the floor. There are no boundaries in the drill, and there is no stoppage of play because of fouls. Aggressive play should be stressed. The drill is usually run for a set number of baskets (6-10 suggested) or a set time limit (3-5 minutes suggested).

Coaching Points:

- Besides conditioning, this drill can also provide an excellent opportunity for players to practice the transition from defense to offense and vice versa.

- Competition can also be added by allowing winners to stay on the court, giving losers additional conditioning activities, or establishing a double elimination tournament.

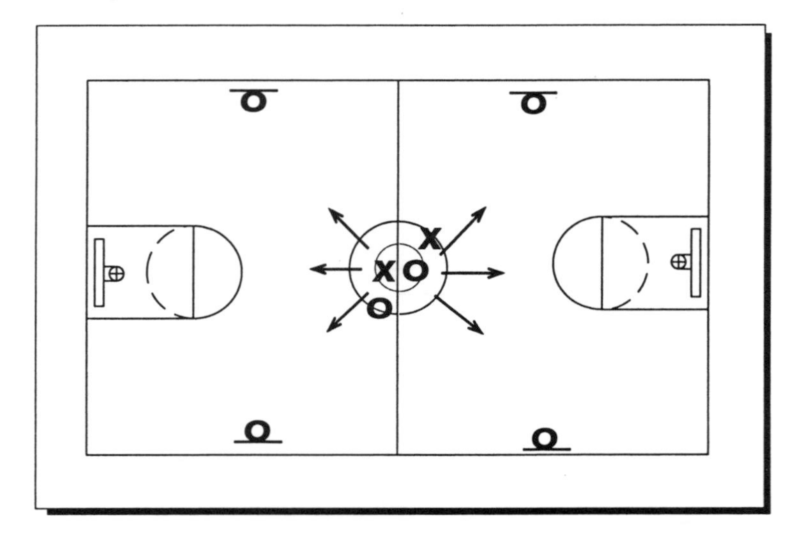

Drill #101: Four Corner Conditioning

Objective: To enhance conditioning and to develop aggressiveness.

Description: Divide the team into four groups and position each of the groups in the four corners of the full court. The first player in each of the four lines participates in the drill. The players coming from the same end of the court are teammates. The coach begins the drill by tossing a basketball into the center of the court. The action signals the four players to sprint to the ball and attempt to score a basket at the opposite end of the court. As soon as one tandem twosome gets the ball, the other two players go on defense. Play continues until one of the two teams scores a basket. There are no boundaries; and play does not stop because of a foul. When a basket is scored, the scoring team goes to the end of the two lines at that end of the floor, while the team that was scored upon sprints the length of the court to join the lines at the other end of the floor. This arrangement helps to keep the lines balanced throughout the entire time of the drill.

Coaching Points:

- For maximum conditioning effects, the coach should place the next ball into play as soon as a basket is made.
- Fouling should be controlled to prevent injury, but should be allowed to a certain extent to encourage aggressive play on the part of the players.
- The lines can be divided according to position if so desired by the coach.

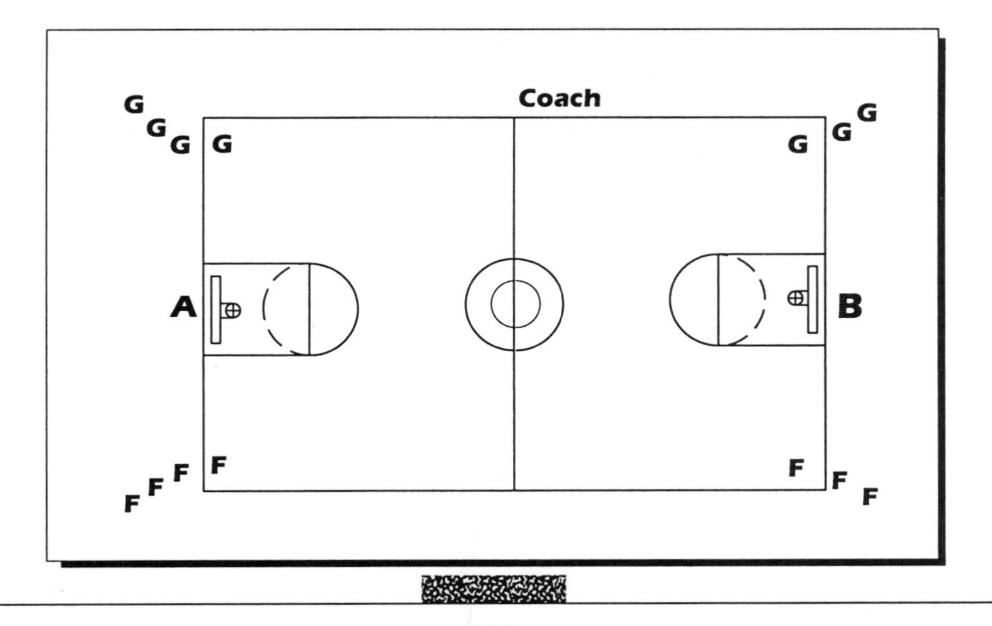

Theresa Grentz is the head women's basketball coach at the University of Illinois. She is the eighth-winningest women's basketball coach in NCAA history, with 474 wins and 170 losses in 22 seasons, including a record of 434-150 in 19 years at Rutgers University. From 1986-94, her Rutgers team made nine consecutive NCAA Tournament appearances. Her 1981-82 team went 25-7 and won the AIAW national championship. In addition, she coached the 1992 U.S. Olympic team to a bronze medal in Barcelona. She has won four National Coach of the Year awards and is one of the original founders of the Women's Basketball Coaches Association. Grentz lives in Champaign, Illinois with her husband, Karl, and two sons, Karl, Jr. and Kevin.

Gary L. Miller is currently the Associate Director of the Division of Campus Recreation at the University of Illinois, Urbana-Champaign, and serves as the editor of the *National Intramural-Recreational Sports Association Journal*. He earned his Bachelor of Science degree in Business Administration from the University of Illinois in 1970. Upon his return from service in Vietnam he earned his Master of Science degree in Recreation from the University of Illinois in 1974. He completed his Doctor of Philosophy degree in Physical Education from the University of Southern California in 1983. *101 Women's Basketball Drills* is his second book. Dr. Miller has spent 27 years working in the field of recreational sports at California State University - Northridge, the University of Michigan, and the University of Illinois. He was an assistant women's basketball coach for three years while working at California State University - Northridge. He lives with his wife, Kathleen, and two children, Erin and Matthew, in Mahomet, Illinois.